Day by Day with God

ROOTING WOMEN'S LIVES IN THE BIBLE

MAY–AUGUST 2011

Christina Press
BRF
Tunbridge Wells/Abingdon

Distributed in Australia by:
Willow Connection, PO Box 288, Brookvale, NSW 2100.
Tel: 02 9948 3957; Fax: 02 9948 8153;
E-mail: info@willowconnection.com.au

Distributed in New Zealand by:
Scripture Union Wholesale, PO Box 760, Wellington
Tel: 04 385 0421; Fax: 04 384 3990;
E-mail: suwholesale@clear.net.nz

Acknowledgments

Scripture quotations taken from The Holy Bible, New International Version, copyright © 1973, 1978, 1984, 1995 by International Bible Society. Used by permission of Hodder & Stoughton Publishers, a member of the Hachette Livre UK Group. All rights reserved. 'NIV' is a registered trademark of International Bible Society. UK trademark number 1448790. • Scripture quotations taken from The Holy Bible, Today's New International Version, copyright © 2004 by International Bible Society. Used by permission of Hodder & Stoughton Publishers, a member of the Hachette Livre UK Group. All rights reserved. 'TNIV' is a registered trademark of International Bible Society. • Scripture quotations taken from The New Revised Standard Version of the Bible, Anglicised Edition, copyright © 1989, 1995 by the Division of Christian Education of the National Council of the Churches of Christ in the United States of America, are used by permission. All rights reserved. • Scripture quotations from the Contemporary English Version © American Bible Society 1991, 1992, 1995. Used by permission/Anglicizations © British and Foreign Bible Society 1997. • Scripture quotations from THE MESSAGE. Copyright © by Eugene H. Peterson 1993, 1994, 1995. Used by permission of NavPress Publishing Group. • Scripture quotations from the Holy Bible, New Living Translation, copyright © 1996, 2004. Used by permission of Tyndale House Publishers, Inc., Wheaton, Illinois 60189. All rights reserved. • Scripture quotations taken from the New King James Version of the Bible copyright © 1979, 1980, 1982 by Thomas Nelson, Inc. All rights reserved. • Scriptures taken from The Amplified New Testament copyright © 1958, 1987 by The Lockman Foundation. Used by permission.

Printed in Great Britain by CPI Bookmarque, Croydon

Mixed Sources
Product group from well-managed forests and other controlled sources
www.fsc.org Cert no. TT-COC-002227
© 1996 Forest Stewardship Council

Contents

Contributors

Tracy Williamson, an author and speaker, is part of Marilyn Baker Ministries, bringing a message of hope and assurance of God's love.

Lyndall Bywater is the national prayer co-ordinator for the Salvation Army. She is a Spring Harvest speaker.

Diana Archer, married to an Anglican vicar in Southampton, is the author of *Who'd Plant a Church*, a warts-and-all account of church planting.

Wendy Bray is a freelance writer, speaker and communications coach. She has two adult (already?) children and lives in Devon, where she is a member of Emmanuel Church, Plymouth.

Bridget Plass travels and performs with her husband Adrian, supports World Vision and speaks at BRF quiet days.

Alie Stibbe works in Business Support at a college of further education. She is also a freelance writer and translator.

Rosemary Green is active in her local church, in which she leads a pastoral care team. She has 14 grandchildren.

Anne Le Tissier is a freelance writer and speaker, seeking to teach, encourage and equip Christian discipleship and also to engage with cynical unbelievers.

Sandra Wheatley trained as a nurse. Though no longer able to work, due to MS, she lives a full life through an extensive prayer and email ministry.

Liz Pacey has worked as a nurse and midwife and with visually impaired people. Currently she writes, studies theology and ministry, and is a reader in the Church of England.

Fiona Barnard is a staff member of Friends International and TEFL teacher. She works with international students and encourages local Christians to reach out in friendship and witness.

Jean Watson is a writer, a spiritual director and a director of a local counselling service. Her work has included teaching, editing and writing.

Catherine Butcher edits the Mothers' Union magazines *Families First* and *Families Worldwide* and has edited *Day by Day with God* since 2003.

Catherine Butcher writes…

The letter writer James was blunt: 'Faith by itself, if it has no works, is dead.' As he explained, 'Show me your faith apart from your works, and I by my works will show you my faith' (James 2:17–18, NRSV). We all know that actions speak louder than words.

Some churches are wonderful expressions of Jesus' love in practice. They run soup kitchens for street sleepers, housing programmes for vulnerable adults and holiday clubs for children. They are generous and gracious, welcoming all. Others are known more for their Bible teaching, for expressive worship, for intercessory prayer or their support for mission around the world. All are important. Together we are a glorious expression of Christ's body.

Within our churches, each of us has different gifts to contribute. Some have more practical skills, and we are each given spiritual gifts of prophecy, teaching, administration and so forth, to build up the church. We need each other to present the whole gospel.

This year, churches throughout the UK are joining forces under the banner of Hope Together to show, both in words and in action, that knowing Jesus brings hope to individuals and whole communities. The key to this initiative, which gave it such success in 2008 as Hope 08, is the commitment of churches working together to demonstrate their faith.

Day by Day with God aims for a similar ethos. Daily Bible reading and prayer are like food and air to Christians—vital for life. But this is not simply a cerebral exercise: our aim is for *Day by Day with God* readers to live lives that are rooted in the Bible, so that everything we do springs out of our relationship with the God revealed to us in the Bible and through the life of Jesus. That's why I always ask contributors to give examples from everyday life. We expect the Bible to speak into the life of each reader and, from your letters, we know that God is applying the words on the pages to specific situations in your lives.

As you use these daily devotional notes and prayers, expect God to speak to you, and look for his prompting to put your faith into action as you share God's love with those you meet, in words and through simple acts of kindness.

Who you are in Christ

Therefore, if anyone is in Christ, there is a new creation: the old has gone, the new has come… God made him who had no sin to be sin for us, so that in him we might become the righteousness of God.

I'm excited to explore the theme 'Free to be you'. All of us hunger to be freer in certain areas of our lives and God delights to satisfy this desire. Part of our journey into freedom is to understand that Jesus has truly removed the 'old' and broken its control over our lives. Our search for freedom need never be a desperate struggle on our part, because Jesus has already done everything necessary to restore our lives. Now he seeks to work in partnership with us to make that freedom real and personal.

But if we are a 'new creation', does it mean that everything that made me 'me' is now blotted out? Not at all! Remember, you were made in his image. Right from the beginning he wove unique and lovely things into the fabric of your life, and this is what Jesus came to restore.

Imagine yourself as a beautiful painting that God, the artist, delighted in creating. Satan, the saboteur, scribbled graffiti, seeking to defile as much of God's handiwork as he could. Satan thought he'd succeeded, but he forgot that God loved what he had created and would do anything to restore it to its uniqueness and glory. This is the powerful work of love he is doing in our lives right now, freeing us from Satan's schemes so that we can be all that God made us to be.

I sometimes watch TV programmes showing art restorers at work on old pictures and antiques. I am always moved and challenged by their belief that under all the damage there is something worth bringing to life again. Their patience, perseverance and attention to the tiniest details of colour and shape are an amazing picture of God's loving, ongoing work in you and me.

....

Lord Jesus, thank you that you died so that I may be free. Thank you for the loving, restoring work you are doing in my life. Please help me to see myself as the beautiful painting you've created me to be, and to learn to live in the truth of it. Amen

TW

You will be called by a new name

For he chose us in him before the creation of the world to be holy and blameless in his sight. In love he predestined us to be adopted as his children through Jesus Christ, in accordance with his pleasure and will.

I was teaching on Isaiah 62 about the new name that God gives us. I then gave the group some listening time. Later, I asked Linda if God had given her a new name. She said, 'Well, something did come to mind but I'm sure I made it up.' I asked her what it was and she diffidently said, 'Chosen One'.

At that moment, God gave me a vision of a garden centre. He was searching through the aisles for something special. One particular tray of seedlings held a picture of the beautiful flowers that the seeds were destined to become. With great joy he said, 'This is my Chosen One. This one will truly reveal my beauty and fragrance and bring me great delight.' I knew then that Linda had indeed heard the Lord. I wrote the vision down for her. She read it and looked stunned, then wrote something back to me. It was my turn to be stunned! She wrote that during recent prayer ministry, the minister had had a prophetic word for her but hadn't understood what it meant. Linda hadn't known either, so had set it aside. Now all was clear. The word was 'garden centre'. How wonderful of God to speak and then confirm his word so lovingly!

God wants you to see yourself truly, as he sees you. He has a special name that expresses both his love and his wonderful purposes for you. You are not just a role, such as a wife or a nurse. Nor is your name 'Failure' or 'Victim'. You are his Chosen One, the one he loves and died for. He has adopted you as his beloved child and chosen bride. This is your true identity. Believe it, think about it and speak it out. It is the truth that frees you.

....

God gives us each a new name (Isaiah 62:2). Where once we might be 'Wounded', we are now 'Healed'; 'Outcast' becomes 'Friend of God'; 'Fearful' becomes 'Confident', and 'Depressed' becomes 'Joyful'. What new name has God given you?

TW

Free of cultural control

'Martha, Martha,' the Lord answered, 'you are worried and upset about many things, but only one thing is needed. Mary has chosen what is better, and it will not be taken away from her.'

I return repeatedly to this story of Martha and Mary and its timeless message. It describes a sibling conflict that we can all identify with, whether or not we actually have siblings. It raises questions. What are my priorities in life? What directs me in the choices I make? Do I feel compelled to act in certain ways? Do I live for people's approval? Are there things I long to do but never try because of other urgent calls on my time? Am I resentful towards others who seem to be freer?

For me, the answer is often 'yes', and maybe it is for you, too, if you are honest. When we live by fulfilling the expectations of others instead of expressing our own unique voice, we, like Martha, can become stressed or resentful. We lose our peace because we are not living out of the wellspring of intimacy with God but in the desert of 'should' and 'ought to'.

Mary chose to listen to her heart and not to be bound by others' expectations. She claimed a right that many people of her time would not even acknowledge because of her sex: the right to hear Jesus for herself. She was secure and free in her choice. She recognised that her desire was a holy desire, honoured by God.

Do you take time to acknowledge your own desires, give voice to your longings and know that God himself put them there and blesses them? It is vital to do this. My spiritual life blossomed the year I followed my heart's desire to go on a silent retreat. As I am a charismatic, many people expressed surprise at my choice, but I knew what I needed. Afterwards I was more whole and in love with Jesus than ever before and newly empowered in my calling to help people grow in intimacy with God.

....

Help me, Lord Jesus, to be true to the person you've made me to be—not to live solely to meet others' expectations but to know my own heart and the unique desires you've put there. Help me to embrace the Mary side of me without fear. Amen

TW

Deceptive 'freedom'

The younger one said to his father, 'Father, give me my share of the estate.' So he divided his property between them. Not long after that, the younger son got together all he had, set off for a distant country and there squandered his wealth in wild living.

The story of the prodigal son challenges us to look afresh at the things that drive us, the illusive 'freedoms' that we desire but that ultimately rob us of peace and contentment. Like the younger son, I sometimes feel, 'My life is so restricted. I need to grab my freedom. I want to experience new things before it's too late. I want to see the world and have excitement!' Similarly, I've mistakenly perceived 'freedom' as something I'd have if things in my life were different: 'If I wasn't deaf; if my family were different; if I was married... I'd fulfil my destiny.'

You may think, 'I'm not driven. I only want what the Lord wants,' but, as Jeremiah teaches, 'The heart is deceitful above all things... Who can understand it?' (Jeremiah 17:9). None of us is exempt from such heart-pulls. The problem is not that we feel them but that we don't recognise them as the deceptions they are. We can even spiritualise them under the guise of passionate faith, perhaps saying, 'If my church wasn't so legalistic, I'd pray for miracles...'

All of these situations may be real, but where is our focus? Freedom does not come from change in external circumstances but from the qualities we develop in our hearts. Paul said, 'I have learned the secret of being content in any and every situation... I can do everything through him who gives me strength' (Philippians 4:12–13).

Are you like the prodigal son, desperate for something more in your life? Don't discover the hard way that changing your circumstances won't bring you more freedom. True freedom is found in contentment, which comes from knowing that you are beloved and already have all of heaven's resources in your grasp.

....

Lord Jesus, thank you for challenging me to look honestly at what misconceptions may be driving me. Thank you that you give me the true freedom of being loved and trusted with your resources. Please teach me the secret of being content in all circumstances. Amen

TW

I am accepted, I am forgiven

But while he was still a long way off, his father saw him and was filled with compassion for him; he ran to his son, threw his arms around him and kissed him. The son said to him, 'Father, I have sinned against heaven and against you. I am no longer worthy to be called your son.' But the father said to his servants, 'Quick! Bring the best robe and put it on him.'

This story shows the father's love and forgiveness releasing his son from the stranglehold of shame. Guilt, shame and a sense of worth-lessness shrivel us inside, stealing our hope and well-being. We live in a pit of apology, constantly rehearsing our badness. We long to be loved but our very demeanour shows that we expect to be rejected.

Jesus told this story because he wanted to show the depths of the Father's compassion. No one understands the pain of guilt and shame better than God does. No one could ever do more to free us from its torment. He took the agonising weight of it all upon his own back, so that we could be healed. Thus we see the father constantly hoping for his son's return, then passionately embracing him, interrupting his confession with words of joyful acceptance and throwing a party for him. Do you know that he does the same for you?

Maybe you too are in a dark place, carrying a heavy weight of shame and regret, constantly telling yourself, 'I'm not worthy.' Do you approach God like a slave, trying to earn peace by doing enough good works? I was there once, too, full of self-hatred. I cried to him to change me. Suddenly I had a vision like Rembrandt's painting of the prodigal son, but *I* was being embraced by the father. I tried to pull back and saw that my dirtiness had marked him. I was astounded when he wept and his tears washed away every mark, on him and on me. His tears made me completely clean and beautiful. He made me a daughter again, and he does the same for you.

....

Father, thank you for your incredible compassion. Thank you for accepting me and making me clean. Thank you that, because of Jesus, I am free of all guilt and shame. Please help me know this in my heart and live fully in the truth of being your daughter. Amen

TW

Freed from the stigma of our pasts

'You did not put oil on my head, but she has poured perfume on my feet. Therefore, I tell you, her many sins have been forgiven—for she loved much…' Then Jesus said to her, 'Your sins are forgiven.'

Today we will look more deeply at shame and at the way Jesus, as our defender, lovingly heals us not just from shame but also from its stigma. Here is a powerful story of a woman who had 'lived a sinful life' (v. 37) and been judged accordingly. Her longing for freedom was deep, but there was no one she could confide in. Yes, she was guilty, but so were others in their condemnation of her. How many harsh rejections and cruel actions had she endured? The stigma of being a 'sinful woman' was inescapable.

Now, though, an anticipatory gratitude was already surging through her, compelling her to gatecrash the religious leaders' dinner and pour out her heart to Jesus with tears and expensive perfume— literally her life savings. A broken and contrite heart, Jesus could not refuse, and never can. Just as he responded tenderly and compassionately to her, so he does to you.

I, too, bore shame stigmas. My years of childhood sexual and verbal abuse were another person's sin, but I carried the pain of it. Inability to communicate, love, hug or look people in the eye were its legacy, along with a crippling heart conviction that I was rubbish.

You need the same passion of trust that drove that woman to Jesus. Drink in these stories and personalise his willingness to defend and forgive the weak, to speak out on their behalf. Know that he does the same for you. Will you dare to push your way in and pour out your soul to him? I did, and he wonderfully healed me—and continues to do so. As I write, I know he is saying to someone reading this, 'The old things have gone, my beloved. Lift up your face to me. "All beautiful you are, my darling; there is no flaw in you"' (Song of Songs 4:7).

....

I am amazed at your love for me, dear Lord Jesus. Help me to rise up in the freedom of knowing that I'm your beloved.

TW

11

Breaking the power of negative words

'Ah, Sovereign Lord,' I said, 'I do not know how to speak; I am only a child.' But the Lord said to me, 'Do not say, "I am only a child."'

How do you talk about yourself? Young mums sometimes say, 'I don't work. I'm just a mum.' That phrase 'I'm just…' reveals their belief that because they are not paid for their work, they have no worth. This is a lie from Satan, based on the false cultural perception that only those who earn money have real value. God says otherwise, that we are precious and honoured in his sight just for who we are.

Do we realise the effects of what we think and say about ourselves? Our words are powerful, and by them we can be bound or set free. 'The tongue has the power of life and death, and those who love it will eat its fruit' (Proverbs 18:21). 'Loving it' means considering our words, choosing to express truth and life rather than negativity. Such 'loving' brings the fruit of freedom and wholeness to our lives and relationships. I often introduce myself with the words, 'I'm Tracy, I'm deaf.' In theory, I'm just letting people know that it will be difficult for me to hear them. In reality, though, I'm speaking out something hidden but heartfelt, and destructive to the truth of who I am in Christ. Like Jeremiah with his plea of youthfulness, I am seeing my deafness as something that makes me too inadequate to be used by God. Other negatives I often speak out are, 'I'm failing… I'm boring… I'm silly.' Such self-talk inevitably allows room to Satan to keep attacking me and binding me up.

God said to Jeremiah, 'Do not say, "I am only a child"', and he says the same thing to you and me. God says that we are his beloved children and heirs, not weaklings or failures. As he told Jeremiah (v. 5), God says that he chose us before we were born and created us for a special purpose.

....

Forgive me, dear Father, for allowing negative thoughts in my heart and for speaking them out. I choose today to renounce Satan's lies and begin to speak your truths. Please open my ears afresh to hear your words of life. Amen

TW

Living in partnership with God

[God] sent the Spirit of his Son into our hearts, the Spirit who calls out, 'Abba, Father.' So you are no longer slaves, but God's children; and since you are his children, he has made you also heirs.

Yesterday we saw how God lovingly rebuked Jeremiah for speaking negatively. What happened next in that story provides more clues as to how we can live in freedom. Jeremiah was told not to fear people because God would protect him. Instead, he should listen and respond to God's daily guidance. God then touched Jeremiah's mouth to release his prophetic gift and gave him a supernatural authority that made his youth irrelevant.

Living in freedom is all to do with practising new, positive ways of speaking, believing and living out our faith. As Paul told the Galatians, God didn't call them just to believe nice ideas, but brought them into a partnership with himself. In that partnership, God gives and we receive; God speaks and we listen and are changed; God anoints us and we then minister in power as his sons and heirs.

I was shocked when God once personalised these truths to me. I was in a restaurant with an unfamiliar group of women. I felt inferior because of my deafness and kept thinking how boring I must appear, while they were so witty. Suddenly God asked me why I was staring at my plate all the time. I told him that I felt rubbish compared to the others, and he said, 'How can you believe that when you're with the king? You're a princess. They can make jokes but they don't know me. Look behind their laughter and I'll show you how to pray for them.' I was stunned! Throughout the rest of the meal, I sensed Jesus with me and heard him whisper in my heart things to pray for the others. I felt such a joy that I was privy to this secret, working in partnership with my Jesus to bring blessing to the very women I had feared. I left with my head up, a royal princess.

....

Father, thank you that you've given me all I need to live in freedom and in power. Thank you that you've made me your child and your heir. Draw me close, Lord, and help me live in true partnership with you. Amen

TW

God frees you from parental rejection

'There is still the youngest,' Jesse answered, 'but he is tending the sheep.' Samuel said, 'Send for him…' Then the Lord said, 'Rise and anoint him; he is the one.'

God believes in you and has created you for a purpose that only you can fulfil. In this story, God rebukes Samuel for the humanly directed way in which he expected to recognise the new king. God said, 'The Lord does not look at the things people look at. Human beings look at the outward appearance, but the Lord looks at the heart' (v. 7). God looks into your innermost being—not just to see if we have hearts to worship him, but because he is searching to bring to life all the spiritual gifts and natural traits he planted in our lives, which equip us to fulfil his calling. The fact that he looks within to the real you is wonderful news in your search for freedom and fulfilment.

God's rebuke freed Samuel to seek the new king from a true perspective, to search with godly understanding and vision rather than fallible human judgment. Just as God was working to release David into his royal destiny, so he wants to release you into yours. David's own father, Jesse, had dismissed the idea that David might have any importance, because he was just the youngest, who would spend his life tending the sheep. Later glimpses show that David's brothers were equally rejecting of their younger sibling. In the eyes of the people closest to him, he was nothing.

Maybe your family has given you the same negative message. I certainly experienced it myself, and it imprisoned me for many years. 'Lazy', 'mental' and 'unlovable' were words I constantly heard. Such judgments from our loved ones are destructive and can cripple our sense of being. But God's word of truth is far more powerful, not just to free you but to make whole the real you, whom God made in love and always delights in as he gazes upon you.

....

Father, thank you that you look upon me truly, not following the negative judgments of human beings. Set me free from the power of all those judgments, Lord, that I may fulfil the destiny you've created me for. Amen

TW

Forgive as the Lord forgave you

'I cancelled all that debt of yours because you begged me to. Shouldn't you have had mercy on your fellow servant just as I had on you?'

God longs to heal our wounds but he cannot work with hard hearts that cling, like limpets, to their right for repayment. The servant owed the king a fortune and, when he faced prison, he begged for time to repay everything. The king took pity on him and cancelled the debt altogether. How amazing! It is inconceivable that such a powerful king should go beyond what his thieving servant begged for and cancel the whole debt. In the story, though, the king did do this, just as God does for us. We, too, have had our whole debt cancelled. Jesus knew that we could never repay it ourselves. He had compassion on us and forgave us everything.

I can hardly believe that this servant would then respond so harshly to the servant who owed him just a few pence, assaulting him and throwing him into prison. How could he? But one day Jesus spoke to me: 'You are that servant. I had mercy on you and cancelled your debt, but you are holding others to ransom for their much smaller debts. Through your unwillingness to forgive, you've locked yourself into a prison of bitterness.'

I was shaken! I'd never thought that I, who loved Jesus, could be like that wicked servant, but I knew Jesus was right. I was in a prison. I'd actually been blaming the devil and the hurtful people in my life. I'd never realised it was my own stubborn refusal to forgive as he forgave me that was holding me there.

God is so merciful. The moment I said sorry and asked for his help, he gave me all the strength I needed to forgive and let go. My prison opened and I started to experience true healing. He will do the same for you. The power of his love in us is amazing.

....

Oh Father, thank you for your forgiveness. Please forgive me for being so unforgiving to others. I choose to forgive them and let them go. Please melt my heart with your love and release me from my prison. In Jesus' name, Amen

TW

Overcoming the devil and his works

Put on the full armour of God so that you can take your stand against the devil's schemes... In addition to all this, take up the shield of faith, with which you can extinguish all the flaming arrows of the evil one.

Paul told us to be on our guard. The devil is a thief who hates our freedom. He works to steal love and bring bondage and fear.

On my first tour with Marilyn Baker, Jane came to us for help about some relationship problems. As Jane described the control struggles, Marilyn suddenly sensed demonic activity. As she prayed, she 'saw' areas in Jane's life that had given the devil a foothold. She gently asked, and in that moment Jane's whole demeanour changed. Vicious anger poured from her as she screamed and swore. Realising that this wasn't Jane but the manifestation of evil, Marilyn and I prayed against Satan in the name of Jesus, encouraging Jane to speak out the truth that she belonged to Jesus and was a temple of the Holy Spirit. We also encouraged her to release God's forgiveness to anyone who had hurt her. Following more Holy Spirit discernment, Marilyn spoke specifically against a stronghold of conflict. With that, as quickly as it had manifested, it departed, leaving Jane exhausted but beautifully at peace. We heard later that all her relationships were in the process of being healed, and she was full of joy.

Do you have patterns of thought and behaviour in your life that, whatever you do, you can't change? Maybe Satan has built up some strongholds that you need to be released from. Jesus has given you his holy weapons of authority and protective armour. Take time to ask God how you can use each part of the armour effectively. Are you protecting your heart with the truth of your righteousness? Do you wield faith, surround yourself with truth and stand on his peace? Do you claim salvation healing over your thought-life?

....

Lord Jesus, thank you that nothing can hold me in bondage or steal my freedom, because you have given me all I need to be free from the devil's schemes. Show me how to use your armour so that my life may be changed and set free. In Jesus' name, Amen

TW

Making your own choices

'Look,' said Naomi, 'your sister-in-law is going back to her people and her gods. Go back with her.' But Ruth replied, 'Don't urge me to leave you or to turn back from you. Where you go I will go.'

There are always people who will advise us. Their counsel may be very wise and well intentioned, and it is important to listen because God may guide us through them. God has not created us to be islands but parts of a body working together. However, for some of us, seeking others' counsel can become a means of abdicating responsibility for our own choices. Every opinion we hear can make us more fearful of even finding out, let alone trusting in, our own ability to hear God and to know what our hearts are telling us.

Ruth was not afraid to listen to her heart and form her own opinion as to what she should do. The two daughters-in-law both heard Naomi advise them to return to their own people, to give them the best opportunity of remarrying and having children. Orpah responded to Naomi's counsel, but Ruth heard a different voice in her own heart—the voice of sacrificial love. This voice said that it was more important to stay close to the one she'd come to love as her own mother than to follow the way of good sense.

Ruth was neither arrogant nor cowed in her decision-making. She obviously respected Naomi with all her heart and yet she respected herself, too. She believed in herself enough to know that her own heart was directing her in the right course of action for herself, and, as much as she respected anyone else, that was the voice she needed to follow. It was listening to and following her heart that ultimately brought Ruth the wonderful reward of marrying Boaz and becoming part of the genealogy leading to Jesus. Awesome!

....

'Beloved one, you have been mocked in your opinions, and I see how you now let them fall to the ground rather than be mocked again. But I have given you the mind of Christ and your heart is my home. Do not be afraid, beloved one. Dare to see and love yourself as I see and love you. Dare to listen to your heart and you will know the reward of my peace and blessing.'

TW

You are unique

If the ear should say, 'Because I am not an eye, I do not belong to the body,' it would not for that reason cease to be part of the body. If the whole body were an eye, where would the sense of hearing be? … The eye cannot say to the hand, 'I don't need you!' And the head cannot say to the feet, 'I don't need you!'

A key to living in freedom is recognising that God made you as you are for a reason. You are not a mistake. Nothing in you, whether it's your body, your thought-life, your spirit or your soul, takes God by surprise. You were created in love for a divine purpose, and that purpose includes even the weak areas of your life.

Do those weaker aspects embarrass you, as Paul describes in his picture of the body? Sometimes we see others and think, 'If only I had Sarah's rapport with children' or, 'If only I was extravert like Karen' or, 'If only I didn't have this disability, I could be used by God.' The thing is, while we are thinking negatively about ourselves, those areas are still there, still part of us—and also part of the body of Christ, as Paul so graphically points out. We can't erase them by wishing them different, but we may paralyse their proper use. Think of that ear, wishing it was an eye. It's still there in the body as an ear, but how effectively is it listening if it's spending all its time moaning that it's not an eye?

Once, when I was feeling very low about myself, God spoke to me. The whole of what he said was quite long, but one phrase stuck out: 'Child, accept the gift I've made you to be.' I was shocked and dismissed it. 'It's Jesus who is the gift,' I thought. But I couldn't forget those words. Eventually, as I prayed, I realised that if I reject part of myself, I reject Jesus working through me. Yes, he is the gift, but he lives in me so that others will also know the gift of his love. Accepting my uniqueness, in both my frailty and my strengths, opens the door for others to meet Jesus.

....

Thank you, dear Father, that you made me unique in all my strengths and weaknesses. Forgive me for rejecting those parts of myself that I haven't liked. Thank you that you are always working your purposes out in me. I choose to accept the gift you've made me to be. Amen

TW

Worshipping in spirit and in truth

'A time is coming and has now come when the true worshippers
will worship the Father in spirit and truth, for they are the kind of
worshippers the Father seeks.'

Jesus' conversation with the Samaritan woman shattered all conventional understandings of worship, and his message is as true now as it was then. What matters is the revelation of love—being known and loved by God and empowered to know and love him in return.

Do you know this joy in your own worship? Have you ever been told that your worship style is wrong, or that your church is too formal or too experiential? Have you ever dismissed someone's favourite hymn as ancient, or rejected liturgy as boring? Does that woman who describes everyone falling under the power of the Holy Spirit send you running for your Bible teaching group?

I, too, have been judged and, sadly, have judged others. My first church was a charismatic fellowship. As a new Christian, I quickly believed its message that any denomination that failed to manifest such freedom in worship was dead. When I started ministering with Marilyn Baker, I was shocked to find how much people loved Jesus even in those so-called 'dead' churches! I repented of my attitude, realising that God didn't care what worship style or songs were used. What he cared about was whether or not people were meeting in love and hunger to know him more. The very diversity of traditions portrayed a much richer picture of the immensity of God's character.

Today I am a charismatic Christian who loves the Holy Spirit's ministry, but I am equally at home in a traditional church with hymns and liturgy, or on a silent retreat. I love lively songs, raising hands, prophesying and singing in tongues. But I also love the awe of an organ-led choral chant or the reverent healing of Holy Communion. Each is an expression of who I am and draws me closer to God.

....

*Forgive me, Lord, for judging others in their way of worshipping you.
Lord, I also choose to forgive those who have made me feel afraid
or inferior about the way I worship. Thank you for calling me to
worship you in a way that reflects my uniqueness. I love you, Lord.*

- TW

As Tracy Williamson has highlighted, it is important to 'be yourself' as a child of God, not trying to mimic others. However, like breathing, eating and drinking, prayer is not an optional extra. Jesus taught his disciples to pray and showed by example that prayer—talking to his heavenly Father—was his priority. He took time to pray, even when he was busy. He got up early to spend time away from the crowds, talking with his Father, and when his disciples asked him about prayer, his response was not 'If you pray...' but 'When you are praying...' (Matthew 6:7, NRSV).

Paul commanded, 'Pray continually' (1 Thessalonians 5:17, NIV). Just as the priests ministered in the temple night and day, our role is to intercede for the world, bringing prayers like an offering into God's presence. Like the Old Testament priests, we bring the needs of the world before God's heavenly throne. We are the 'royal priesthood' that Peter described in his letter (1 Peter 2:9).

Over the next two weeks, Lyndall Bywater will be taking us through a study on intercessory prayer. As Tracy has reminded us, God wants us to be ourselves. We each have a unique part to play in the kingdom of God. There will be people, issues and insights that are uniquely ours to intercede about.

If you read reports from mission organisations around the world, particularly those in contact with Christians in countries where churches must meet in secret, there are regular stories of people who discover Jesus without any contact from believers. Jesus comes to them in dreams and visions, answering their longings. Could these encounters be in response to intercession from around the world for these 'closed countries'?

Throughout the next fortnight, ask God to prompt you through the day to recognise the people and issues he wants you to be interceding about. This side of eternity, we might not know how God has answered our prayers, but pray confidently, knowing that he delights to give good gifts to us, his children.

Intercessory prayer: starting simple

'Keep on asking, and you will receive what you ask for. Keep on seeking, and you will find. Keep on knocking, and the door will be opened to you. For everyone who asks, receives. Everyone who seeks, finds. And to everyone who knocks, the door will be opened.'

It was my dad's turn to preach in church. He did it often, and, being a fairly normal child, I was usually much too bored with adult church to listen to him properly. But on this occasion he got my attention. You see, he mentioned the 'cake plate'.

The cake plate was a family tradition of ours. A tempting selection of little cakes would be arrayed on a plate and put on the tea table. You could only have two cakes from the plate, so we would each be asked to choose which two we would like. My dad, in a moment of shining paternal pride, triumphantly informed the congregation that, no matter what cakes were on the plate, he always knew which two his only daughter would pick. The story caught my attention because it was about me, but he went on to make a point about prayer, which I immediately understood and have never forgotten. He explained that, no matter how sure he was about which cakes I would choose, he still always waited for me to ask for them.

Today we begin two weeks of study on the theme of intercessory prayer. We will look together at scriptures from Genesis to Revelation, to discover what the Bible has to say about how we pray for others. It's a subject that raises many questions along the way, but we begin by reminding ourselves of some simple and comforting truths.

Your loving heavenly Father knows his children. When you come to him in prayer, he knows what you will choose to ask him for. He could pre-empt you and save you the bother of praying at all, but the truth is that he values your freedom and loves to hear your voice, and so he waits for you to ask.

....

Whose voice do you love to hear? What emotions does it stir in you when you hear it? Take a moment to reflect on the truth that your voice evokes those emotions in the Father's heart when you speak to him in prayer.

LB

A labour of love

May He grant you out of the rich treasury of His glory to be strengthened and reinforced with mighty power in the inner man by the Holy Spirit Himself indwelling your innermost being and personality.

Don't you just love listening to children pray? This prayer, from a collection of children's prayers that I found some years ago, always cheers me no end: 'Dear God, I didn't think orange went with purple until I saw the sunset you made on Tuesday. That was cool!' (Eugene)

We adults have a tendency to overcomplicate prayer. We worry about what words we're using, whether our theology is strictly correct, whether we should say 'In Jesus' name' at the end or whether God will just know we meant it that way all along. Before we know it, prayer has become an art rather than a heart. It's prayers like Eugene's that cut through our adult complexity and remind us what it's really about. There's no art to it, the theology is base-level, and there's not a hint of Jesus' name anywhere, but it's all heart. It's the loving overflow of a child's day-to-day journey with God.

Paul had journeyed a long way with the church in Ephesus. Having planted it, he had invested blood, sweat and tears in its early growth. His letter is full of vital foundational teaching for the believers there, but, right in the middle of it all, he breaks into prayer; and that prayer, it might surprise you to know, has an awful lot in common with Eugene's. Yes, it is theologically more complex and linguistically better formed, but at its heart Paul's prayer is, like Eugene's, a simple, deep prayer of love.

Intercession is not about form and content; it is first and foremost about love. We may not have the words and we may not understand the theology, but when our love and longing for others spills over into a heartfelt cry to God, then he leans close to hear us.

....

Have a go at 'decluttering' your prayer language. Pick someone you love and want to pray for, then begin to talk to God about them, making your language as everyday as possible. Make your prayer as simple and heartfelt as you can.

LB

Intercession is partnership

'The person who trusts me will not only do what I'm doing but even greater things, because I, on my way to the Father, am giving you the same work to do that I've been doing... From now on, whatever you request along the lines of who I am and what I am doing, I'll do it. That's how the Father will be seen for who he is in the Son.'

I must confess to being rather fond of online shopping. I like few things better than a day spent gloriously lost in retail heaven (so long as there are coffee shops aplenty), but when it comes to necessity rather than pleasure, then I love the facility of being able to load up a website, find what I need in moments, and then click on a button that automatically buys it for me, packages it up and posts it to my house.

The trouble is, I tend to handle intercessory prayer with much the same approach sometimes. The stores of heaven are arrayed before me in spiritual cyberspace, and all I need do is assess the earthly problem, select the heavenly solution, then click on it with a quick prayer and wait for it to drop into my lap.

In his last teachings to his disciples before his death, Jesus talked a lot about intercessory prayer. Over and over again he promised them that they would receive, if only they would pray in his name.

It sounds like the ultimate online delivery experience, doesn't it? You click on a blessing, enter the 'Jesus' password and wait for the download to begin. Yet nothing could be further from Jesus' mind. For him, intercessory prayer is about partnership. He is the first and greatest intercessor (Hebrews 7:25; Romans 8:34). His life's work is the reconciliation and redemption of all creation, and he invites us to join in with him.

Intercession is not clicking on the solution we like best. It is looking to see where Jesus is working, and then joining our own prayers to his cause.

....

Jesus, thank you for the gift of prayer. Thank you for the privilege of partnering with you. Today, help me to see where you are working and what you are doing, then help me to tune my prayers to chime in with your heart. Amen

LB

Intercession is worship

'If you abide in Me, and My words abide in you, you will ask what you desire, and it shall be done for you.'

What you want in life is generally dictated by what you worship. If the most important thing to you is financial stability, then your desire will probably be for a well-paid job or a win on the lottery. If your primary goal is popularity, then you will prize the good opinion of others more than anything else in life. In fact, if you're interested in checking out what you're worshipping, try asking yourself what it is that you really want at the moment.

When it comes to intercessory prayer, what we want becomes a rather important factor. Our prayers are the overflow of our hearts, as we have already seen, and it is mighty difficult to pray truly for something that you don't truly want. If our worship is askew, then so will our desires be; if our desires are askew, then our prayers will be ineffective.

I am eternally comforted by the fact that Jesus knows us so well. Today's reading is another part of his final instructions to his disciples before his death, and it touches on the tricky issue of our wants and our worship. It's a deeply compassionate talk: he knows how flawed we are; he knows that our tendency will be to disconnect from him and go after other sources of fulfilment. But it's also a stern warning: if we turn aside from the only true source of life, we will become unfruitful.

Jesus follows that connection through into our prayer lives, too. If he remains the object of our worship and we stay connected to him, then we will find our prayers being answered. Why? Because when we worship the right thing, we want the right things. When we want the right things—the things that are best for us and for others—then he is delighted to deliver.

....

Is there a prayer you've been praying, which you know comes from misplaced worship in your life?

James 4:1–3 shows us one reason why our prayers might not be answered.

LB

Intercession is authority

'I tell you the truth, you will ask the Father directly, and he will grant your request because you use my name. You haven't done this before. Ask, using my name, and you will receive, and you will have abundant joy.'

Travel on the London Underground is a truly self-esteem-boosting experience for me. Being blind, I need assistance to travel on routes that I don't already know, so I present myself at the ticket gates and ask the member of staff there to radio for someone to escort me. And so the cry rings out across the station radio network: 'Gateline to Base: assistance requested for a VIP!' OK, so VIP actually stands for 'visually impaired person', but just for a moment or two I bask in the glory of being some kind of celebrity!

Jesus is nearing the end of his final teaching now, and an infectious joy bubbles up in his words. He can see the cross but he can also see the day when he will ascend victorious. Excited by what is to come, he exhorts his followers to grasp their place in the order of creation. In him, they have VIP access to the Father himself.

Many of us still live a rather 'Old Testament' prayer life. We're so aware of our shortcomings that we can hardly believe that God even listens to our prayers, let alone gives them any weight. We approach him apologetically, pleading with him to give ear to our requests and hoping he might grant one or two of them, if we've made the grade.

Nothing could be further from the truth. The picture Jesus paints is of his own brothers and sisters—beloved adopted children, made right with God—walking humbly but confidently into the Father's presence and asking him to supply what is needed for the work of his Son's great kingdom. To be heard in heaven, we don't have to make the grade or pray the best prayer. We just have to show up in the throne room. Because of Jesus, we have VIP status there.

....

Reflect on how you see yourself as you approach God. Are you a hesitant, apologetic supplicant or an adopted, confident co-heir with Christ?

Read Hebrews 10:11–15 to get a glimpse into the throne room.

LB

A question of character

'Will you sweep away the righteous with the wicked? What if there are fifty righteous people in the city? … Far be it from you to do such a thing—to kill the righteous with the wicked, treating the righteous and the wicked alike. Far be it from you! Will not the Judge of all the earth do right?'

Have you ever seen a friend of yours do something really out of character? Maybe someone you know to be entirely placid has given way to road rage, for instance. It's as though you have to do a double-take, isn't it? You suddenly find that everything you thought you knew about the person has shifted by several inches.

Abraham was getting to know God by now, but on this occasion he had to do his own double-take. The God of grace and justice, who had shown himself to be kind and compassionate, seemed to be planning to destroy a city, regardless of the fact that God-fearing members of Abraham's own family lived there. So Abraham began a dialogue with God, which counts as perhaps the first example of intercessory prayer in scripture. His starting point was God's character. He knew him to be a God of justice, and he used that knowledge as the basis for his prayer, calling on a just and fair God to act on his character by not punishing Abraham's innocent loved ones.

Perhaps the most wonderful aspect of this story is God's response. Far from smiting Abraham for his audacity in calling him to account, he seems to welcome the dialogue. It is as though he was challenging Abraham to get involved—to speak up on behalf of his loved ones.

Sometimes in life we need to pray difficult prayers. It's as though God is acting distinctly out of character: the people we love are hurting, and it offends us. Take heart from Abraham's story. God loves the dialogue. He invites us to call on him to act on his character, and he loves it when we speak up passionately in prayer for those we love.

....

Read Psalm 145, and note some of the things it says about the character of God. Then choose several people in your life who don't seem to be experiencing those good things from God at present, and speak up to God on their behalf.

LB

Intercession can be ear-bashing

Then the Lord said, 'Learn a lesson from this unjust judge. Even he rendered a just decision in the end. So don't you think God will surely give justice to his chosen people who cry out to him day and night? Will he keep putting them off?'

No matter how many years I spend studying and teaching the topic of prayer, there is one element of the subject matter that I still grapple with. I may spend several hours enthusing to a whole crowd of people about the miraculous effects of intercessory prayer, but I am just as likely to be weeping in frustration, five minutes after the end of the session, with someone whose deepest and most desperate prayer has not been answered. I know too many people who, when faced with Jesus' question about whether the just judge keeps putting people off, would say, 'Yes, in my experience he does.'

Today's story has several different interpretations, but for us it is an echo of yesterday's story from Genesis. Jesus is echoing Abraham's description of the God of the universe as the 'fair and just judge', and he seems to be suggesting that God simply cannot be untrue to his nature by failing to deliver justice for those in his care. So where does that leave us when he seems to fail to live up to his own standards?

Strangely enough, the virtue that Jesus seems to appreciate most about the widow in the story is her ability to nag. How many men have ever extolled that particular virtue in their nearest and dearest women? Yet, for Jesus, it is a strength, and he even implies that nagging is a kind of faith. (You may like to try that, the next time someone tells you to stop nagging!)

The just judge may not have delivered for you yet, but he urges you to stay in the dialogue with him. He will bring justice for you in the end—his character does not allow him to do otherwise—but in the meantime he welcomes you to nag him as much as you need to.

....

Is there a prayer you've stopped praying for fear of becoming a nag? Sometimes God tells us to stop asking because it is done, but, if you haven't heard him say that, he would be delighted if you would keep nagging him, please.

LB

Shoulders and heart

'Whenever Aaron enters the Holy Place, he will bear the names of the sons of Israel over his heart on the breastpiece of decision as a continuing memorial before the Lord.'

Emily laid her teddy bear aside and knelt down. 'Mummy,' she said, 'can we do short prayers tonight?' Perplexed, Emily's mum asked, 'What do you mean by short prayers?' 'Ones where we skip all the boring relatives and just pray for the puppy I want you to buy me,' replied Emily, with a cheeky grin. Let's be honest, shall we? There are certain prayers that are easier and more enjoyable to pray than others. Maybe it feels unholy to admit it. Let me assure you, though, that, if you have sympathy with Emily, then you're probably quite normal.

God gave Moses a very specific design for the priestly garments that he wanted Aaron and his family to wear. They weren't fashion items; they were representations of the priest's vocation, so each part of the design had some relevance to the job the priest was doing.

One of the priestly tasks was to bring the Israelite people before God in prayer, and so God required the priest to wear the names of the tribes of Israel inscribed on stones and attached to his clothing. That way, every time he entered God's presence, he carried every tribe in with him. Instead of having the names attached just once, though, God instructed that they be attached twice—once on the shoulders and once over the heart. You see, God knew his priests well. He knew that praying for their people would sometimes be a passionate, heartfelt experience, and sometimes it would be more like shouldering a burden.

It is entirely normal for prayer to be both those things. There are Emily's boring relatives—the things we have to pray for but don't find particularly inspiring—and then there's the new puppy, the things we pray for with ease and passion. God hears and values them all.

....

If you keep a daily prayer journal, why not make sure you're covering a good mix of heart and shoulders each day—things you find it easy to pray for and things that are more of a discipline? That way, prayer will stay fresh and fruitful.

LB

Shoulder burdens

I urge you, first of all, to pray for all people. Ask God to help them; intercede on their behalf, and give thanks for them. Pray this way for kings and all who are in authority so that we can live peaceful and quiet lives marked by godliness and dignity.

Breakfast with my parents-in-law is an impressive experience, not just for the food but also for the prayer time. Beside the toast and jam, there is usually a small but comprehensive pile of prayer diaries, letters from missionaries and daily reading books. Once we've eaten, we work our way through these missives, gathering the topics for prayer, and then we bring them before God together. Breakfast in my house is a less impressive affair, especially when it comes to prayer. I am usually half asleep, and am liable to forget to pray for anything beyond the thing that is most preoccupying me for the day ahead.

Paul is preparing young Timothy for church leadership, and one of the first injunctions he gives him, as he outlines the responsibilities of a leader, is to ensure that certain types of prayer feature regularly in the life of every believer. In our experience-hungry society, we might naturally assume that they should be things like 'powerful worship' or 'deep meditation', but in fact Paul is talking about something much more mundane. He is talking about praying for our leaders.

Last week, we read Jesus' words about working in partnership with him. That partnership exists not just for our personal fulfilment but for the well-being of the community, region and nation in which we live. As a fellow intercessor with Christ, I am expected to make space in my prayer life to pray for those who lead and influence the world around me. Yet, praying daily for our MP or local councillors is rarely a matter of passion for most of us. It is a burden we choose to shoulder. It takes discipline and the daily willingness to look out beyond our own needs and our own cereal bowls to the world beyond.

....

Wise and all-powerful God, today I pray for those in leadership in my community—my MP, local councillors and all those in leadership in education and health. Grant them understanding of the issues we face, and integrity to make fair choices as they lead. Amen

LB

Matters of the heart

The Lord heard Elijah's cry, and the boy's life returned to him, and he lived.

The prayer meeting was progressing well. The 15 or so people were sitting in a circle, heads bowed at an appropriately prayerful angle, voices dropped to a suitably reverent *sotto voce*, and the prayer points on the overhead projector were being diligently and methodically processed. All was well.

Then, suddenly, Mrs Whitaker went off-message. Sitting up straight in her chair, she took a deep, lung-bursting breath and began to rant. Not for her the prayerful whisper; not for her the fourth point down on the list. No, she began to call out at the top of her voice, asking God to heal her grandson's leukaemia. The effect on the prayer meeting was radical. Suddenly it had life.

God required the tabernacle priests to wear the names of the tribes of Israel over their hearts. He didn't just want them to acknowledge the needs of their people formally in prayer; he wanted them to bring a heart-cry for their nation into his presence.

Elijah must have been getting used to seeing miracles by this point in his ministry. Ravens had brought him food, and a pot of flour had lasted far longer than it should have done. So we might think that the unexpected death of the widow's son wouldn't have fazed him much. But it did, and he was helpless. At this moment of deepest distress, what broke from his lips was not a formal, ordered prayer but a heart-cry, and it was the heart-cry that returned the answer from heaven.

We sometimes worry that expressing our deepest feelings in prayer might be considered immature or out of control. Yet God wants us to pray from our hearts. He expects us to be deeply moved with passion and compassion for those around us, and he wants to hear our heart-cry.

What is your heart-cry at the moment? If you were only allowed to pray one more prayer for the rest of your life, what would that prayer be for?

Read Galatians 4:19 to see how Paul describes his passion for the Galatian believers.

LB

A feisty fight

Next to him was Shammah son of Agee the Hararite. When the Philistines banded together at a place where there was a field full of lentils, Israel's troops fled from them. But Shammah took his stand in the middle of the field. He defended it and struck the Philistines down, and the Lord brought about a great victory.

I got knocked over by a goose once. It was early one Easter Day, and I was on my way to morning worship at a certain well-known Christian conference, when a Canada goose flew right at me and knocked me over. I can only assume that it must have been a nesting female, and that the presence of my guide dog had caused her alarm. She left me in no doubt as to how far she would go to protect her little ones.

Today's reading may strike you as rather unusual, but I include it because it features one of my biblical heroes. He only gets two verses but he inspires me, especially when it comes to intercessory prayer.

The warrior Shammah had taken up his position in a lentil field. Even after the rest of the army had abandoned it and him, he refused to let it go. Why? We have no idea. It was a dangerous and seem-ingly futile escapade, but he didn't count the cost. He didn't do a risk assessment, he just stood his ground. He fought for it until he didn't have to fight any more.

Do you have a lentil field? Is there something that raises a fighting spirit in you when you pray for it? Is there something you are standing for at the moment, and you know you won't leave your position until God has brought breakthrough? If that is you, then can I encourage you to hold your ground today? Intercessory prayer has often had me defending lentil fields—fighting on in prayer, long after everyone else has gone, for something that seems ludicrously impossible and even a little crazy. Yet I take heart from Shammah. He stood his ground, and, as a result of what he did, God brought about a great victory.

....

God of the angelic armies, please give me your strength for the fight today. When I'm discouraged, renew my courage; when I'm weary, increase my resolve; when I'm fearful, help me to look to you. I ask for the power to stand here and fight until victory has been won.

LB

Dangerously life-changing

The king said to me, 'What is it you want?' Then I prayed to the God of heaven, and I answered the king, 'If it pleases the king and if your servant has found favour in his sight, let him send me to the city in Judah where my fathers are buried so that I can rebuild it.'

The 24–7 Prayer movement sprang up in 1999, when a church full of young people in Chichester, West Sussex, decided to set aside a room in their church building for one month of non-stop prayer. They figured that God had provided thousands of ways for them to communicate with him, so the room was a feast of creative ideas, beautiful art and blank spaces for people to express themselves. Having thought that a month of 24–7 praying would be a hard slog, they were surprised at how easy it was to fill the hour-long slots. The place was saturated with God, and people wanted to be there.

Yet the effects were much more long-term and life-changing than even these dreamers could have believed. From that prayer room, and from many others like it, people have gone out into the world to do astonishing things for God. Pete Greig, one of the first in that Chichester prayer room and one of the founders of 24–7 Prayer, coined this phrase to sum up what intercessory prayer should mean for us believers: 'Pray as if it all depends on God, and live as if it all depends on you' (*Red Moon Rising*).

Nehemiah had a prestigious job and a rather nice life… until he began to pray. I often wonder whether he knew where he would end up, when he started praying for his desolate homeland. And I wonder when it dawned on him that he was to be the answer to his own prayers. He himself would rebuild the ruined defences of Jerusalem.

God is looking for people who are prepared to let their prayers turn into action. Prayer isn't a get-out clause; it's a promise to partner God in his work, no matter what that involves for us.

....

Have you been praying for something and begun to hear God call you to action on it? If so, what is the first thing he is asking you to do?

LB

Modern-day temples

'Now my eyes will be open and my ears attentive to the prayers offered in this place. I have chosen and consecrated this temple so that my Name may be there for ever. My eyes and my heart will always be there.'

I recently visited the UN building in New York. One of the Secretaries General of that amazing organisation had decided that their head-quarters should have a meditation room, to reflect the importance of spirituality at the heart of humanity. Being something of a fan of prayer rooms, I was keen to check it out.

I can say with some conviction that it was one of the most soul-less places I have ever visited. It was interesting, and even beautiful in its own way, but all it resonated with was the good intentions of a human being.

David longed to build a temple for his God, and God refused to let him do it. When he finally agreed to let Solomon fulfil David's dream, he made one thing very clear. Whereas the worshippers of other deities built temples for their gods to live in, the chosen people should never be led to believe that the true God could be confined to dwelling in a habitation built by humans. The temple would be a dwelling for his name, not his being.

This knowledge makes God's promise on the day of consecration of the temple even more remarkable. He would not and could not dwell in it himself, but he promised that two aspects of his being would always be there: his eyes and his heart.

The temple is gone, but the promise is eternal. When we set aside a space to meet with God—be that a room in our church or a time in our day—he promises that his eyes and his heart will be there. He will see us; he will understand our struggles and our joys. But more than that, he will give us access to his heart.

....

Next time you set aside a space to pray, remember God's eyes and his heart. Thank him that he loves to meet your gaze. Invite him to share his heart with you.

Read 2 Chronicles 6:18–21 to learn Solomon's understanding of God's dwelling place.

LB

It's all about the future

I heard a voice thunder from the Throne: 'Look! Look! God has moved into the neighbourhood, making his home with men and women! They're his people, he's their God. He'll wipe every tear from their eyes. Death is gone for good—tears gone, crying gone, pain gone—all the first order of things gone.'

'Intercessory prayer is spiritual defiance of what is in the way of what God has promised. Intercession visualises an alternative future to the one apparently fated by the momentum of current forces. Prayer infuses the air of a time yet to be into the suffocating atmosphere of the present. History belongs to the intercessors who believe the future into being' (Walter Wink). To be an intercessor, you've got to be a dreamer. When everything around you stays stubbornly unchanged, persistently unhealed, frustratingly unfulfilled, there's only one thing that keeps you on your knees, and that's the ability to imagine that one day it could all be different.

The book of Revelation is not, first and foremost, a treatise on how the world will end. It is a call of encouragement to a battered and beleaguered church. The believers were being persecuted, and the heady days of Pentecost must have seemed a far-off memory, so God sent them a story. It's full of magnificent and strange creatures and cataclysmic events, but its message is fantastically vivid: 'Don't forget, it won't always be this way. One day it will all be different!'

In my experience, the quality that people prize most in intercessors is our ability to go on believing, even when everything seems hopeless. As we draw our studies on intercessory prayer to a close, let me bring you the challenge of the dreamer: no matter how unanswered your prayers may look, don't give up praying them unless God tells you to. Your highest and most exciting calling as an intercessor is to believe the future into being.

....

Revelation 21 is John's vision of his 'home city', once the presence of God has thoroughly invaded it. Why not write something similar for your local community? What would the homes, streets, businesses and churches look like if God's kingdom really did break in?

LB

Over the past two weeks, Lyndall Bywater has encouraged us to take steps as intercessors. It is because Jesus is always interceding for us (Hebrews 7:25) that we can have a relationship with God.

In the next fortnight, Diana Archer points us back to the main focus of our faith: Jesus, as presented to us by his much loved disciple, John.

John described himself as the 'disciple Jesus loved'. He was next to Jesus at the last supper (John 13:23). He stood with Mary, Jesus' mother, at the foot of the cross, and Jesus entrusted Mary into John's care (19:26–27).

John was one of the first disciples to see the empty tomb, to realise that Jesus had risen and to recognise him on the shore of the lake, cooking breakfast while the disciples were out fishing on the lake. John gained unique insights into Jesus' life, grasping the amazing reality that Jesus was both God and man, the one who had made all things and yet walked and talked with friends, and who loved the world enough to die for us.

John has a special understanding of God's love for us, and he appreciated Jesus' use of everyday pictures of water, bread and light, which reveal so much to us.

Take time over the fortnight to read through the whole Gospel of John, asking God to reveal Jesus to you in fresh ways, giving you a deeper appreciation of his love for you and for the world.

Notice the word-pictures Jesus uses and the way he treats women in a culture where women were rarely seen and never heard. Stand in awe of our wonderful Saviour and take time out to thank him for his amazing love.

The beginning

In the beginning was the Word, and the Word was with God, and the Word was God... Through him all things were made... In him was life, and that life was the light of all people. The light shines in the darkness, and the darkness has not overcome it.

There is nowhere better to start delving into the breathtaking world of John's Gospel than right at the beginning, so here we are. It is almost impossible to read these opening words while sitting down: they demand to be announced with gusto. We are plunged straight into the vast canvas of John's understanding of who Jesus was and is, and how he relates to the whole of life, creation, people and God. Not for John the careful genealogy of Matthew, or Luke's historian's perspective. He jumps in with extraordinary claims of eternal dimensions. He sets out an enormous easel, gets out a huge paintbrush, and begins with sweeping brushstrokes to portray for his readers the significance of Jesus Christ. And that's before he even uses his name.

John's first vibrant colour reminded his Jewish readers of the first words of Genesis: 'In the beginning...' They would also have understood the 'Word' as a reference to God. His Greek readers would have understood it as 'reason', the rational principle behind everything that exists. Thus, with one stroke, John spoke to two people groups. More extravagant strokes drew in creation, followed by light and life, connecting them together in 'all people'. The Word is the light that enlivens all creation, including Jews, Gentiles, you and me.

This canvas really is massive. There are no edges to it, no limits. In a few short sentences, John paints a picture of the whole world, from its creation to its meaning. And he has us hooked because he uses words that are familiar to us, too. We all know about light and life and darkness. We all wonder about God. Like many who 'begin' with John's Gospel, we want to see the rest of the picture.

....

How do you talk to others about   Read 1 Corinthians 9:19–23 to
Jesus? Are there ways in which   see how Paul tackled this issue.
you could use more of their   DA
language rather than your own?

The meaning

From the fullness of his grace we have all received one blessing after another. For the law was given through Moses; grace and truth came through Jesus Christ. No one has ever seen God, but God the One and Only, who is at the Father's side, has made him known.

John piles more paint on to his enormous picture of God, the universe and everything, but he puts in many colours before he ever mentions Jesus' name. He paints in John the Baptist first (I imagine he would be blue, with all that baptising), whose clear purpose was to testify to the 'light'. He puts in the bright, luminescent colours of life, light, creation and glory, all as depictions of the 'One and Only'. He adds the mixed shades of invitation and rejection, the colours of a world that does not recognise the incarnation of its Creator. He splashes on the surprising news that those who do recognise and believe in him can become 'children of God'. He tells us what he is like, long before we know his name. Finally, the Word is defined as Jesus Christ.

Unlike the impersonal 'rational force' of Greek understanding, Jesus is revealed as personal, the ultimate expression of a glorious God, bearer of grace and truth. Truth proves to be a dominant colour in the rest of the Gospel, mentioned 25 times. John really wants his readers to understand that this is it—this is what the world is all about. Subsequent to the gift of the law through Moses, now there is blessing, grace and truth through Jesus. Not only that, but we can know him, in a way we could never know an impersonal force.

There is so much stashed into these few verses, it is hard to take in. It's the meaning of life! John invites us not just to wonder at the picture he has painted but to step right into it. Will we choose to believe, again and again? Will we define our understanding of life, truth, meaning and creation wholly through the 'One and Only... full of grace and truth' (v. 14)?

....

How would you put what you believe about the truth of Jesus into your own words? Or into your own picture?

See Ephesians 1:3–12 for Paul's depiction of the meaning of life.
DA

Belief

'For God so loved the world that he gave his one and only Son, that whoever believes in him shall not perish but have eternal life. For God did not send his Son into the world to condemn the world, but to save the world through him.'

When we look at the picture that John paints for us in his Gospel, as well as light, life and truth, another important colour is 'belief'. The word occurs 98 times, and even someone like me, who is generally unimpressed by statistics, can see that that makes it significant. Of course, it also gives rise to the most famous verse in the New Testament, quoted above.

Jesus was talking to the Pharisee Nicodemus when he said these words. John records their conversation in detail. Jesus appears almost exasperated with this Pharisee who has come to him at night to chat. Why did Nicodemus choose the night-time? Was he afraid of the crowds? Did he just want a decent amount of time to talk without interruption? Tantalisingly, John does not tell us. But Nicodemus' comprehension was certainly darkened, too. Jesus spelt out for him and us what it means to be 'born of the Spirit'. It's all to do with belief.

This is something that most of us know very well, but sometimes we lose sight of who we are believing in; and what eternal life actually is. I can easily get caught in the trap of thinking that I have to do all the saving myself—both of myself and of others. Instead of living in the security of the fact that God loved the world so much, and that Jesus has saved the world, I behave as if I have to prove myself worthy of it. That's really not the point at all. The challenge is to throw myself into belief—belief that Jesus has done it all and is big enough even for my complicated self, belief that I can live as if I were born of the Spirit every day of my God-given, eternal life.

....

Dear Father, thank you for sending your Son. Help me to abandon myself in trust of your complete saving power. Amen

Read Deuteronomy 33:26–29: God has always been saving.

DA

Signs and wonders

A second time they summoned the man who had been blind.
'Give glory to God,' they said. 'We know this man is a sinner.' He
replied, 'Whether he is a sinner or not, I don't know. One thing I
do know. I was blind but now I see!'

Many people in our churches are fascinated by miracles, or 'signs
and wonders'. These are generally understood to be occurrences
that are unexplainable except for the divine action of God. Debates
rage over whether they still happen, with some insisting that miracles
wereconfined to the first century, and others telling miraculous stories from today. It is a contentious subject and feelings run high.

It was very similar in Jesus' day. The crowds ran after Jesus because
they had heard he did signs and wonders: 'Unless you people see
miraculous signs and wonders, you will never believe,' he says in
John 4:48. However, John recorded the signs he saw for one purpose
alone. John 2:23 says, 'Many people saw the miraculous signs he was
doing and believed in his name.' The once-blind man in today's passage testified, 'Nobody has ever heard of opening the eyes of a man
born blind. If this man were not from God, he could do nothing' (vv.
32–33). All the questions we ask can be found in this man's story—
questions of authenticity, authority, method, sin and fault—but the
vital factor for John was that the glorious 'wonders' performed by
Jesus demonstrated who he was, and challenged onlookers to make a
choice. Each of these stories of signs and wonders—whether healing,
feeding 5000 people or raising the dead—end with the same question: will the onlookers believe in Jesus?

John chose his narrative carefully, focusing on stories that would
present people with this choice. The signs are all there. If Jesus is the
same yesterday, today and for ever, what signs point you, me and others to belief today?

....

Father, open my eyes and my
heart. Help me to see you at
work in miraculous ways in my
world today. Amen

Read Genesis 15:5–6: it all
started with one man's belief.

DA

I AM

Thomas said to him, 'Lord, we don't know where you are going, so how can we know the way?' Jesus answered, 'I am the way and the truth and the life. No one comes to the Father except through me. If you really knew me, you would know my Father as well. From now on, you do know him and have seen him.'

Believing in Jesus is the key to John's picture of the meaning of life. Another way this is expressed is through the 'I am' sayings of Jesus— the ones I am always tempted to cherry-pick whenever I go anywhere near this Gospel. In John's portrayal, they are bright, deep, eye-catching concentrations of colour that stick in our minds: 'I am the bread of life (6:35)... the living bread (v. 51)... the light of the world (8:12)... the gate for the sheep (10:7)... the good shepherd (v. 11)... the resurrection and the life (11:25)... the true vine' (15:1). Many of them appeal to deep longings within us—for life, truth, provision, direction and light. 'I am' recalls the name of God in the Old Testament, familiar to the Jews (see Exodus 3:14), while words such as 'way', 'truth' and 'life' would have resonated with the Greeks. So perhaps it is not surprising that we are drawn to these 'sayings', when they are so intellectually and emotionally rich.

Jesus promises extraordinary things through himself. He promises that through him we will know the Father. He promises that he is what we need in life. Which of the sayings jumps out at you, and why? For me, today, it is that Jesus is the 'the good shepherd'. I love the thought that he is watching out for me, challenging me to higher, richer pastures and checking that I am on the right path. Yet I understand Jesus as a shepherd because I have been a Christian for years. Jesus used illustrations from the world around him, so what would more contemporary alternatives be? I am the reliable bank? I am the only life assurance you need? What do you think?

....

Take some time to relate to Jesus as the good shepherd—or whichever 'I am' resonates with you today.

DA

Water into wine

**Jesus and his disciples had also been invited to the wedding…
Jesus' mother said to him, 'They have no more wine.' 'Dear woman,
why do you involve me?' Jesus replied. 'My time has not yet come.'
His mother said to the servants, 'Do whatever he tells you.'**

When we look closer at the picture John paints, we see that many
of the detailed stories he tells involve women. The first woman who
appears in the Gospel is Jesus' mother. How reassuring! Despite the
fact that there are no stories about Jesus' birth or background in John,
his mother is here. This story comes straight after Jesus' meeting with
John the Baptist by the River Jordan and his calling of the first few
disciples, but nothing else has happened yet. It is just the 'third day'
after John the Baptist has identified Jesus as the Son of God (1:34).

So here they are, enjoying a social occasion, and Jesus' mother
puts him on the spot. Just how did Jesus speak to his mother: what
intonation did he use? His reply hints at a fascinating relationship
between his mother and himself. Presumably she knew about his
'time'—the time for his identity to be revealed, the time for him to
demonstrate the nature of God's kingdom, the time for his ultimate
showdown in Jerusalem. What conversations had they had? His
mother knew that she could confidently point the servants in his
direction, to solve the embarrassing problem of the lack of wine.

Jesus' first miracle in John's Gospel was done to rescue a party.
The jars were filled with water on his instruction, and were then
found to contain the best wine of the feast. There are many elements
that make this a brilliant beginning to Jesus' ministry—from the inter-
play with his mother to the extravagant provision for celebration, to
the practical nature of his actions, to the affirmation of humanity and
marriage and community, to the suggestion of the party waiting for us
in heaven… to the smile that Jesus brought to the faces of the guests.

....

*Dear Father, when life is tough, it is easy to lose sight of Jesus'
affirmation of parties and celebrations. Help me to rediscover what it
means for my life that you turn water into wine. Amen*

DA

41

Water into eternal life

Jesus answered, 'Everyone who drinks this water will be thirsty
again, but those who drink the water I give them will never thirst.
Indeed, the water I give them will become in them a spring of water
welling up to eternal life.' The woman said to him, 'Sir, give me this
water so that I won't get thirsty…'

Here is woman number two in John's picture—a Samaritan. Bearing in mind John's careful reminder that Jews considered Samaritans 'unclean' (v. 9), it is extraordinary that Jesus chose not only to talk to her but also to ask her for a drink. Using a Samaritan utensil would have made Jesus ritually 'unclean': he would have had to purify himself afterwards by washing in a *mikvah*, a pool kept for that purpose.

Jesus did not have to go through Samaria. He could have chosen a different route. But his encounter with the woman was clearly all part of God's plan.

Despite the fact that Jesus was hot, tired and thirsty, he engaged the woman in a wide-ranging debate covering faith, worship, political issues, the Messiah, eternal life, and her own chequered marital history. It was not until he revealed his knowledge of her life story that he really had her hooked. She tested him out even then, asking questions to find out whether she really had met the One who would change the way she thought, believed and worshipped, for ever. But once she was sure, she rushed off and dragged people out to see Jesus. Because of her belief, many Samaritans became believers in Jesus the Messiah. When they saw that result, the returning disciples must have had their answer to why Jesus was breaking all the rules that day (v. 27).

Jesus gave the woman respect, attention, challenge—and himself. He started where she was, engaged with her questions, but led her on to truth. This is how he treats you, and how we should treat others.

....

Dear Father, I want the water   Read Jeremiah 2:13 to learn
you promise. I want that spring   what not to do.
inside me, welling up to eternal
life. I want to be able to offer it   DA
to others. Lead me into truth.

Second chance

Those who heard began to go away one at a time, the older ones first, until only Jesus was left, with the woman still standing there. Jesus straightened up and asked her, 'Woman, where are they? Has no one condemned you?' 'No one, sir,' she said. 'Then neither do I condemn you,' Jesus declared. 'Go now and leave your life of sin.'

Jesus' actions and words were causing trouble between him and the leaders of the Jews, especially the conscientious Pharisees and the teachers of the law. Opinion was divided as to whether he was good or bad, a blessing or a curse. Many of the ordinary Jewish folk were drawn to him, though, and writing him off was not an option. So the woman discovered in the act of flagrant sin was a perfect opportunity for the Jewish leaders to trap Jesus: perhaps they would find something to condemn in his reaction.

As usual, Jesus reacted in a totally unexpected way. He knelt down, drew on the ground and invited anyone who was without sin to cast the first stone. Mel Gibson's film *The Passion of the Christ* (2004) portrays what happened next especially powerfully, as the dropping stones clatter on the dusty ground. The cowering woman reaches out slowly for Jesus' feet, but he bends down, takes her hand and helps her to stand. Her dirty, beaten face dares to look up at his, and she finds no condemnation there.

In the middle of intense personal challenge, Jesus sidestepped the leaders' antagonism and showed compassion to the woman. She was in the wrong, but she was given a second chance. It is horribly easy to get caught up in condemnation, of ourselves and of others. We want the rules kept, thank you very much, and we jump on our own failures and those of others far too readily. We can beat ourselves up without any need for stones. We can judge others without compassion. Jesus challenges us to a different way.

....

Imagine yourself into this story. Whether you find yourself holding a stone or crouching at Jesus' feet, take his lead for what happens next.

Read John 21:15–19 to see another second chance offered by Jesus.

DA

Grief and hope

When Mary reached the place where Jesus was and saw him, she fell at his feet and said, 'Lord, if you had been here, my brother would not have died.' When Jesus saw her weeping… he was deeply moved in spirit… Jesus called in a loud voice, 'Lazarus, come out!'

In one of the most moving encounters between Jesus and individual women, he arrives near the home of Mary and Martha, four days after their brother Lazarus has died. Jesus had a long history with these three, visiting their home (Luke 10:38) and loving them all (John 11:5). John records in vivid detail the painful moments of meeting, as Martha blurts out her belief that her brother would not have died if Jesus had been there. Yet Jesus had chosen to stay away (v. 6).

Martha is often remembered for her stressed-out hospitality (Luke 10:40), but I have much sympathy with her. On that occasion, she could not cope with seeing Mary choosing to learn from Jesus' teaching, as a man would, rather than helping with the chores. But here, Martha is the first to welcome Jesus, the first to broach the impossible subject of her brother's death, the first to declare her belief in Jesus as 'the Christ, the Son of God' (v. 27). As she returned to fetch her sister, did she dare to believe also in what might happen next? How did she interpret Jesus' words, 'I am the resurrection and the life' (v. 25)?

Then it was Mary's turn to meet Jesus. Despite knowing what the outcome would be, Jesus cried when he saw her grief. He didn't say, 'There, there, look, it's OK really.' He did not ride roughshod over her feelings. He felt the grief, too. This is a profound moment in the Gospel. It tells us that God cares about all our pain, despite his promises—of a future with him, of resurrection, of a party in heaven where all tears will be wiped away (Revelation 21:4). He can see the end from the beginning, but he is in the moment, now, with us. In our deepest times of despair, we are never alone. Jesus wept.

....

Dear Father, it is extraordinary to think that you cried too. Please help me to be aware of your loving care, and please bring me resurrection and life. Amen

Read Hebrews 4:14–16 for another angle on Jesus' compassion.

DA

House of scent

Here a dinner was given in Jesus' honour. Martha served, while Lazarus was among those reclining at the table with him. Then Mary took about a pint of pure nard, an expensive perfume; she poured it on Jesus' feet and wiped his feet with her hair. And the house was filled with the fragrance of the perfume.

The raising of Lazarus had a severe effect on Jesus' ministry. News of it reached the ears of the chief priests and the Pharisees, and they hastily convened a meeting of the Sanhedrin, the high court of the Jews, seeing the miracle as a threat. If Jesus went on doing these things, it could upset the delicate political balance. The Jewish leaders feared an uprising, which could result in greater oppression by the Romans. This was a justified fear, but it blinded them to the significance of what was happening through Jesus.

The feast that Martha threw in Jesus' honour was held in the teeth of increasing danger and antagonism. Jesus slipped into Bethany while everyone was looking for him in Jerusalem for the Passover. Perhaps the atmosphere was a potent mix of joy, celebration, gratitude and awareness that their time with Jesus could well be limited. It is amazing to think of the once-dead Lazarus 'reclining at the table' with his family and Jesus. And then, out of love and thankfulness and a desire to give something to Jesus, Mary anointed him with the oil.

One of the theological arguments for the authenticity of John's Gospel is the eyewitness detail it contains. Here, John adds the unnecessary information that the beautiful perfume filled the house with its scent. There is no doubt that Jesus valued her gift and took it as a kind of preparation for his coming ordeal (v. 7). Martha fed him; Mary anointed him; Lazarus sat with him. Jesus needed these human touches, just as we do. There are times when I wish I could show my gratitude for what Jesus has done in my life in similar tangible ways.

....

How might Jesus know that you love him?

Read Matthew 25:37–40 for some suggested answers to that question.

DA

Light in the darkness

Near the cross of Jesus stood his mother, his mother's sister, Mary the wife of Clopas, and Mary Magdalene... [Jesus] said to his mother, 'Dear woman, here is your son,' and to the disciple, 'Here is your mother.' From that time on, this disciple took her into his home.

The next time we see women appear in the Gospel picture is at the unforgettable scene of the crucifixion. The combination of Jewish and Roman authorities has manoeuvred Jesus to his death.

It is impossible to imagine how it must have felt for the women mentioned here to watch Jesus die. It is fascinating that they *are* mentioned. Apart from them, 'the disciple whom Jesus loved' (presumably John himself) is the only one named. Perhaps the other disciples were all in hiding already. This seems likely: if I had been there, in such an intense and unlooked-for experience, I would have remembered the names of everyone else who was present. It's almost as if John wants to give honour to these faithful women, who stuck by Jesus to the end. They stuck by each other, as well—two sisters and two friends supporting each other through the unsupportable.

Then came the extraordinary provision of Jesus for his mother, asking John to take her into his home, and giving her a son again, even as he was forced to leave her. In a male-dominated world, Jesus' mother needed someone to care for her instead of him. Perhaps the rest of the family were not yet believers and there was nowhere else for her to go. Whatever the overwhelming emotions and questions of that day, this scene is full of tenderness and care in the midst of calamity—people who stuck by each other, people who thought for each other, and solidarity in the face of unbearable cruelty. The value of true friendship and love can never be overestimated. We are built for interdependence, and when the chips are down, it can be the one thing that gets us through.

....

To whom can you be a true friend today? Who needs a word or action of encouragement? Or do you need to ask for help yourself?

Read Ecclesiastes 4:11–12 to find some friendship truths.

DA

Women first

'Woman,' he said, 'why are you crying?' … Thinking he was the gardener, she said, 'Sir, if you have carried him away, tell me where you have put him, and I will get him.' Jesus said to her, 'Mary.' She turned toward him and cried out in Aramaic, 'Rabboni!' (which means Teacher).

The disciples Peter and John had already run with Mary Magdalene to the tomb to discover that Jesus' body was not there. They saw the burial cloths lying there, and they saw the head cloth folded up separately (another of those details that shouts to us down the centuries, 'I really saw this!'). The two men then left for home, but Mary stayed, weeping her heart out. As if Jesus' death was not enough, now his body had vanished. But when Mary peered into the tomb, she saw two angels in white. She must have wondered what she was seeing, her eyes blurred with tears. Then came the most incredible moment, as she turned, thought she was speaking to the gardener, and finally realised that it was the risen Jesus. It was just as he had said.

So it was Mary who was entrusted with the wonderful news that Jesus was alive again. Every Easter, I try to imagine how it must have been—first, to believe the evidence of her own eyes, and then to convey it to the terrified disciples, both men and women. The other Gospel accounts vary as to exactly which women went to the tomb, but Mary Magdalene is there in all of them. What a privilege to be the first to know, to be so vital to the story that has changed the world!

I visited Jerusalem recently as part of a trip around Israel. There are two contenders for the site where Jesus was crucified and buried, one nearer the place of the Skull (19:17) than the other. It is possible that Jesus was lifted up on a cross in a place that is now a bus station. Who knows if either of the sites is authentic? But, as it says on the inside of the garden tomb door, 'He is not here. He is risen.'

....

Dear Father, help me to live knowing that you are alive. Amen

DA

47

It's all about love

'If you obey my commands, you will remain in my love, just as I have obeyed my Father's commands and remain in his love. I have told you this so that my joy may be in you and that your joy may be complete. My command is this: love each other as I have loved you.'

It was so difficult deciding what to pick out of John's Gospel for these daily notes. As I said at the beginning, the picture he paints for us is simply vast. I have chosen the dominant colours of a few major themes and the fascinating details of the stories involving women, but there is so much more. There are Jesus' teachings, his healings, Jesus walking on the water, clashes with the authorities, the feeding of the 5000… so much colour, texture and nuance to explore. It has been said, purportedly by the fourth-century bishop Augustine of Hippo, that 'John's Gospel is deep enough for an elephant to swim in and shallow enough for a child not to drown.' As I near the end of this brief glimpse at John's canvas, though, there is one beautiful colour that I cannot ignore. This is, of course, the theme of love.

Perhaps love is even more than a gorgeous swathe of gold illuminating the whole picture. Perhaps it is the actual canvas on which the picture is painted, for John is convinced that love is the reason for everything. The love that God has for the world causes him to send his Son. The love that the Father and Son have for each other motivates Jesus' ministry and obedience. It is love that means the Holy Spirit will come and lead believers into truth. It is love for the Father that will keep the disciples together in unity.

In his final words before he was arrested, Jesus emphasised, in as many different ways as possible, that the command to love was the most important imperative he was leaving with his followers. It was the way to union with himself, and to complete joy. It really is what makes the world go round.

....

Dear Father, help me to love and be loved in the way you intended. Amen

Read John 13:1–11 to see Jesus' love in action.

DA

The best bit

From this time many of his disciples turned back and no longer followed him. 'You do not want to leave too, do you?' Jesus asked the Twelve. Simon Peter answered him, 'Lord, to whom shall we go? You have the words of eternal life.'

I have to confess, I have saved the best till last. This is my favourite part of John's Gospel, the best bit in the picture. It comes early on, straight after Jesus has caused upset with his mysterious words about being the bread of life that comes down from heaven. Many of the disciples struggled with this idea. What could he possibly mean? The only heavenly bread they knew about was the manna that God had provided for their ancestors in the desert (6:31). How could Jesus compare with that? Then, when he started saying that they had to 'eat the flesh of the Son of Man and drink his blood' (v. 53), it was all too much. They argued and grumbled. They did not understand, and many of them decided that this was one 'hard teaching' too many (v. 60). It offended them. They left.

There are times when the Christian way seems most unlikely, times when it is hard to believe. There are times when faith is stretched to breaking point, times when suffering is overwhelming. There are times when, frankly, faith is confusing and what Jesus says is hard to swallow. In those times, I remember these verses. I remember Peter's response to Jesus' question, and I know that there is nowhere else I would rather go than to follow Jesus. When evil threatens, I need a mighty name to pray with. When sin spoils, I need a saviour. When life falters, I need something to live for. No one else offers anything anywhere near what Jesus offers. No one else loves like he does. No one else offers himself like he does. No one else died for me. He is the one who has the words of eternal life. There is nowhere else to go.

....

Do you follow Jesus wholeheartedly? Why?

Read John 21:24–25. What is your favourite part of John's Gospel?

DA

A study in John's Gospel is a fitting introduction to the focus of the next week: Pentecost. Of all the Gospels, John's account of Jesus' life is full of the glory, mystery and majesty of our eternal saviour—the only one qualified to announce, 'Before Abraham was born, I am! (John 8:58, NIV).

John made special note of Jesus' explanation of the Holy Spirit's role as Jesus took time over the last supper to describe to the disciples what was about to happen. Jesus knew that the disciples would be troubled and tested to the limit by his death. He reassured them, 'Do not let your hearts be troubled... I go to prepare a place for you... I will come again and will take you to myself, so that where I am, there you may be also (14:1–3, NRSV).

Jesus also promised, 'I will not leave you orphaned... But the Advocate, the Holy Spirit, whom the Father will send in my name, will teach you everything' (14:18, 26).

When you tell toddlers, 'Christmas is coming', they have no idea what you mean, but as soon as they have experienced one good Christmas with presents, great food and lots of fun, they anticipate the next Christmas with mounting excitement.

The disciples didn't have any idea what Jesus was describing to them, but when the Day of Pentecost came and the Sprit was poured out as Joel had prophesied, then they knew. When Paul described the Holy Spirit to the Ephesians, he was able to express more fully what Jesus had explained. The Holy Spirit is like a deposit, guaranteeing our inheritance as children of God (Ephesians 1:14, NIV).

Over the next week, ask God to fill you afresh with his Holy Spirit and look forward to the day when we will see him face to face.

Called to be church: the preparations

'Do not leave Jerusalem, but wait for the gift my Father promised, which you have heard me speak about.'

I am going to ask you to engage your imagination! As we consider the Pentecost that launched the early Church, we will read words that may be familiar to us, but are no less exciting and visionary for that, so we may need a fresh perspective. Try, if you can, to be among this group of Jesus' early followers. Begin here, alongside the risen Jesus as he gives repeated reassurances about what will happen next.

It has been a bewildering, often terrifying few weeks. You are exhausted; you were grief-stricken, yet now you are elated, excited and intrigued. What will this 'power' (v. 8) be like? What makes it so important that Jesus mentions it repeatedly? What part will you play in all this?

There is no suggestion of fear among the group now. Instead you pray together, visit the temple often and, democratically and prayerfully, choose the man to replace Judas (what a promotion that must have been!), adding him to the eleven apostles. Notice that there is order, prayer and authority. For all the excitement of these days, there is no hurrying on with effervescent enthusiasm. Instead, there is confident resolve and a recognition that there is more than a job to do— there is a vocation.

With his repeated reassurance, Jesus inaugurated the last days, the messianic era (the time between his first and second comings). The promise and pouring out of the Holy Spirit were part of that inauguration. This would be a time of the knowledge of God, the outpouring of the Holy Spirit and great witness (v. 8).

We are still living in this time: these were our church beginnings. And, as we'll discover over the next few days, what a beginning it was!

....

What does the insight you have gained from placing yourself in this story suggest to you about how you might live in 'this time'?

WB

Called powerfully and personally

All of them were filled with the Holy Spirit and began to speak in other tongues as the Spirit enabled them. Now there were staying in Jerusalem God-fearing Jews from every nation… Amazed and perplexed, they asked one another, 'What does this mean?'

Are you still with the followers of Jesus in your imagination? So, what happened next? Well, Luke gives a matter-of-fact account. You are together in a relatively public place—maybe the temple precincts. A large crowd of 'God-fearing Jews' is in town for the festival period, from 'every nation under heaven' (v. 5). Suddenly, there is a sound like wind, a sight like fire, and words—lots of them—in many languages, spoken by Peter and the others. You realise that the visitors can understand what is being said, not by sharing a common language of interpretation but because they are all 'hearing' their own native tongues. Understandably, they are excited.

Jeremy Begbie has written, 'Ethnic distinctiveness was not overrun; indeed it seems it was needed. A community of the "unlike" was born' ('The future' in *For the Beauty of the Church*, ed. W. David O. Taylor). That 'community'—the new Church—was universal and multicultural from the very beginning.

To my surprise, while staying in Seattle, USA, I missed hearing English voices among the crowds. When I finally did hear an English accent, I started a conversation with the speaker, who admitted to sharing my sense of loss. How much more wonderful must it have been for these men and women to hear God praised in their own language in a strange city? Our mother tongue is precious to us, and on this occasion it gave special intimacy to the words. Through them, God spoke to the heart by the power of his Holy Spirit.

As men and women of learning (albeit informally), they inevitably asked the question, 'What does this mean?' Peter is about to explain.

....

Why do you think we so often forget how universal and inclusive the Church is and has always been? What can we do about it?

WB

Called in fulfilment of prophecy

'In the last days, God says, I will pour out my Spirit on all people.
Your sons and daughters will prophesy, your young men will see
visions, your old men will dream dreams... And everyone who calls
on the name of the Lord will be saved.'

The Holy Spirit has made his presence felt powerfully and personally
among the people gathered. You are in the middle of the excitement.
It dies down as Peter, standing just above the assembled crowd, with
authority you have rarely seen, gestures for quiet. He has heard the
question 'What does this mean?' and he intends to answer it. 'Let me
explain what is happening,' he says.

Reading this passage today, you may think that the crowds are
in for a very short sermon. Three minutes, perhaps? (Don't we wish
sometimes?) But it was undoubtedly much longer: Luke has included
a mere précis. Peter begins by pointing to the fulfilment of the prophecy of Joel 2:28–32, which is well known by the crowd around you.
'This is biblical,' we might say now. 'Look! Here it is,' says Peter, and
roots the events of the day in what was known, loved and respected
by his audience. This is the Spirit of God 'poured out', he says. It's
not a dribble or a jarful, but an abundant 'glug glug'; a power shower
(not that you are familiar with such things in first-century Jerusalem,
of course!), a drenching—characteristic of God's generosity.

Peter emphasises the fulfilment of Joel's prophecy as illustrated
in the first and final quoted verses (vv. 17, 21). This has happened
so that you—men and women, old and young—may be saved, says
Peter, saved to live a life full of the Holy Spirit. He wants them to
know that the Holy Spirit is not a random force. In yesterday's reading we saw God's Holy Spirit acting personally; here he is purposeful.

But, says Peter, the best way to understand what is happening here
is through Jesus, not Joel. And so his sermon goes up a gear...

---

*Why is it important to remember that the Holy Spirit is always
purposeful as well as powerful?*

WB

Called to be church by 'this Jesus'

'God has raised this Jesus to life, and we are all witnesses of the fact. Exalted to the right hand of God, he has received from the Father the promised Holy Spirit and has poured out what you now see and hear.'

Now, as you stand among the expectant crowd, Peter turns his attention to Jesus, talking about his life and ministry, his death and resurrection. He reminds the crowd that Jesus showed himself to be the Messiah through signs and wonders (v. 22), that he has conquered death and that God 'has poured out what you now see and hear' (v. 33)—the Holy Spirit. Even King David, he says, prophesied that God's saving purpose would be worked out through Jesus' death. That death may have come about through the schemes of evil men but it was also central to the purposes of God. Peter makes old and new faith converge to present the truth to the assembled crowd: they are witnesses to the resurrected Jesus and to the outpouring of the Holy Spirit. The sense of awe and expectancy is almost tangible. How will they respond to 'this Jesus' (v. 36)?

Some time ago, I went through the experience known as 'the dark night of the soul'. I questioned many of the constructs of my faith and tore some of them down. 'Easy answers' and certainty became anathema to me. As I searched through the rubble for what I could believe, I met again 'this Jesus': real, human, unpolished by glossy PR and neat dogma. I realised that I could live within the frayed, uncertain edges of faith if I could live rediscovering the person of Jesus, through his life, his death and his resurrection. I felt as if I was starting again.

Gerard Hughes wrote, 'The resurrection is the finger of God on my scars and a deep breath to start again' (quoted by John Rackley in *The Baptist Times*, 16 April 2010). Those words have great meaning for me. They are, I believe, in essence, what Peter was trying to say.

....

Lord, place your finger upon my scars. Grant me fresh understanding of your death and resurrection, so that I may 'start again' with a deep breath, today.

                                                                                    WB

'What shall we do?'

When the people heard this, they were cut to the heart and said to Peter and the other apostles, 'Brothers, what shall we do?' Peter replied, 'Repent and be baptised, every one of you, in the name of Jesus Christ for the forgiveness of your sins.'

Peter has just finished speaking. He has told the crowd that God has made 'this Jesus' Lord and Christ. He is the one they have been waiting for. Luke says that these words 'cut to the heart' of the people.

As you stand in this crowd, look around at the faces close to you. What does 'cut to the heart' mean for them? Look at their eyes, their facial expressions, their body language. They glance from one to another for clues; they look at you. They mumble, clutch hands or nudge one another. Then they look back to Peter, searching his face for an answer to the question that unites them all: 'What shall we do?' Peter replies, 'Repent and be baptised, every one of you.'

The Jews believed that baptism was only for Gentiles converting to Judaism, so this act would have been, at best, humbling and, at worst, humiliating. But it was necessary. It is not enough for us to be convinced and to believe; we have to act. When things have deep meaning for us, when we engage with them body, mind and soul, we want to do something. That's why hundreds of young people travel overseas on short-term mission projects each year, why William Wilberforce battled in parliament to end slavery, and why organisations such as Faithworks and Tearfund exist.

Has God been calling or nudging you to do or to be something? Perhaps you've been slow to hear, or quick to argue. God doesn't always call us in the way we expect. Sometimes he allows us some discomfort, or perhaps even an inability to hear him. Yet, still, he wants us—like the crowd at Pentecost—to go on listening and to be willing to 'do something'.

....

Ask yourself: what is God calling me to do or to be today? What will be my response? Share your thoughts prayerfully with a wise friend.

WB

'Every one of you'

'Repent and be baptised, every one of you, in the name of Jesus Christ for the forgiveness of your sins. And you will receive the gift of the Holy Spirit. The promise is for you and your children and for all who are far off—for all whom the Lord our God will call.'

As you stand in this amazed crowd, the truth of what they have to do ('repent and be baptised') sinks in, along with the amazing idea that the gifts of forgiveness, grace and the Holy Spirit will be theirs.

So what are you thinking? Be honest. 'But I'm not used to scrutinising a crowd of first-century people!' OK, let's change the scene a little. Imagine yourself in the crowd that is your worshipping community on a Sunday—coffee time, perhaps. Just to make things fun, imagine that the most annoying man you know (yes, that one) is right in front of you. Just over there, by the chocolate biscuits, is her—that woman who hurt you badly all that time ago—along with the one who always talks about you behind your back ('in love', of course).

What are you thinking now? How about, 'What? Even him? He has the Holy Spirit as a gift? And can God really forgive her? Does God know what she's like?' The short answer to all of those questions is yes, yes, yes and yes. And what's even more shocking is that he loves, forgives and has given his Holy Spirit to you—and to me—too!

It's a light-hearted exercise, but with more than a ring of truth to it, wouldn't you say? Because sometimes we forget what Peter makes plain. The gifts of forgiveness and the Holy Spirit are for 'every one of you... for all whom the Lord our God will call'.

As hard as it can sometimes be, it is up to us to bring those faith-filled gifts of grace, forgiveness and the Holy Spirit into our dealings with everyone—the annoying, hurtful and gossiping included. And because God loved and called them first, we might even count it a privilege.

....

Oh dear, Lord God. I am reminded of ....
Help me to forgive and to love in the power of the gift of your
Holy Spirit.

                                                                                          WB

A new community

They devoted themselves to the apostles' teaching and to the fellowship, to the breaking of bread and to prayer. Everyone was filled with awe, and many wonders… were done by the apostles.

The crowd has dispersed, baptisms are under way and now there's the little 'challenge' of what's to be done with the 3000 people 'added to their number'. Commitment to the Messiah means commitment to the messianic community. The task must have been enormous. Three thousand people speaking different languages but making up one multinational community: it makes the organisation of the Olympic Village look easy! But, as we read earlier (1:12–26), the apostles were well organised. They also knew the value of community. We cannot be Christians alone. Community and communion are about more than just celebrating diversity and difference with a happy-clappy time together. They take work, love, self-sacrifice and vision.

So what kind of community did these early leaders endeavour to build? What kind of church was it? Luke gives us a clear model, the elements of which should be the hallmarks of a worshipping community today. It was a learning, loving, praying, sacramental church, enjoying regular fellowship (v. 42). It was an awe-filled and supernatural church expecting God to work wonders (v. 43). (Could it be that we don't experience supernatural wonders because we don't experience awe?) It was a generous (v. 44), relevant (v. 46) and worshipping church (v. 47)—a church that was known and loved, and wanted to make Jesus known and loved.

You and I are still called to be the human building blocks of this kind of community. Our understanding of this account of the birth of a diverse, worldwide church calls us to work for personal and ecumenical unity, through and in the power of the Holy Spirit and blessed with the gifts of grace and forgiveness. Can you imagine that?

....

Lord God, may my understanding of the early days of this 'Pentecost church' inspire me and make me bold in faith, love and forgiveness in my own church, today and tomorrow.

WB

Which are your most special relationships? Best friends? Family? They might be especially close. But neighbours and colleagues—even political allies—might enjoy a special relationship that affords special privileges.

The Holy Spirit is a mark of our special relationship with God. The presence of the Holy Spirit in our lives marks us out as children of God and is a guarantee of our inheritance as part of God's family.

The children of Israel were chosen and marked out by God for a special relationship that models the special relationship we can all have with God because of Jesus. They came to him on the basis of sacrifices offered to atone for their sins. We come on the basis of Jesus' sacrifice, which atones for all our sins.

Our special relationship with God was anticipated by the Old Testament prophets who looked forward to the day when God would pour out his Spirit on 'all flesh', as Joel had prophesied (Joel 2:28–29).

Jesus demonstrated the impact of the special relationship we can have with his heavenly Father. When he was baptised, the heavens were opened; the Spirit of God descended on him like a dove and a voice from heaven said, 'This is my Son, the Beloved, with whom I am well pleased' (Matthew 3:17, NRSV).

Jesus ushered in a new era when God's Spirit makes it possible for us to have a father–daughter or father–son relationship with the Creator of the universe.

Jesus fulfilled the law and introduced a new age of grace, in which it is possible for each of us to stand before God, blameless, with our sin covered by Jesus' blood. So we too can hear God say to us, 'This is my child, my Beloved, with whom I am well pleased.'

Over the next week, Bridget Plass will be looking at fathers in the Bible, as we mark Father's Day. As you meet with God each day, ask him to give you a fresh understanding of the special relationship you have with your heavenly Father as his precious child.

Father's love

When Israel was a child, I loved him, and I called my son out of
Egypt. But as the saying goes, 'The more they were called, the
more they rebelled.' … Israel, I can't let you go… I just can't do it.
My feelings for you are much too strong… I am the Holy God—
not merely some human, and I won't stay angry.

So much passion. So much frustration. So much fatherly disappoint-
ment. God echoes parents down the ages, as they look wistfully
through the photo albums they began when their child was a baby:
'He was such a lovely little boy…'

Whatever books might say, it is jolly hard being a good mother
and, I suspect, even harder to be a good father. Now that my own
children are grown up, I realise that it doesn't necessarily get easier,
just different. There are times when you could cheerfully chuck them
and all their opinions and life choices in the bin, and, if Hosea is to
be believed, God has similar reactions to his son's disobedience and
wilful rejection of everything he has been taught as a child—even to
the point of banishing Israel 'to his room' for endless years of exile in
Babylon. However let down and hurt and even rejected many parents feel, though, most of those I know are still determined to stay
stuck in, even when the going gets tough.

How God's words echo the yearning in every parent to have their
children safely back at home, whatever they have done and however rebellious and self-destructive they have been. I have heard it
said that the story of the prodigal son could never find a place in
the Old Testament. Yet here we have God himself, the Holy God,
saying, 'I can't give you up… I just can't do it.' Neither could we,
Father, neither could we.

....

*Loving Father, as we think about everything we have done and
continue to do—thank you.*

BP

Hedge of hope

Job's sons took turns having feasts in their homes… After each
feast, Job would send for his children and perform a ceremony, as
a way of asking God to forgive them of any wrongs they may have
done… Satan remarked, 'You are like a wall protecting not only
him, but his entire family.'

What a dear old dad Job clearly was, worrying that his kids may inadvertently have upset God, and anxiously but determinedly making
sure that everything was put right. I think it's a parent's prerogative to
try to mop up after their children, to make sure they haven't offended
or upset anyone. It doesn't always work, though.

When our eldest son was two, we went to stay with older relatives who had no children and very expensive furniture. I expect we
nagged him something rotten and curbed every smidgeon of curiosity
and spirit, so afraid were we that he would offend his hosts or destroy
something precious. 'Don't forget to say, "Thank you very much for
having me",' we nagged on the day we were leaving. 'So, what do
you say to Auntie and Uncle?' his dad confidently prompted him as
we stood surrounded by our cases in the hall. Our son took a deep
breath, smiled angelically and said, 'Thank you very much for having
me', followed by (just as loudly and clearly and without a pause),
'There, that's got that done!' Our apologetic parting did little to help.

How reassuring to discover that, in some special way, through
his efforts to make everything right between his children and their
Creator, Job is able to charm God into building a hedge of protection
around his entire family. But then God has always responded to passion, as we see so clearly in Jesus' encounter with Jairus, who cared
deeply enough about his little girl to seek out Jesus and plead for him
to come to his home (Mark 5:22–23). How reassuring to know that
God hears our passionate prayers on behalf of our children.

....

Thank you, Father, for hedging us around with your love and
protection. Nothing can separate us from your love.

                                                                    BP

Jairus' sacrifice

When [Jairus] saw Jesus, he went over to him. He knelt at Jesus' feet and started begging him for help. He said, 'My daughter is about to die! Please come and touch her, so she will get well and live.' Jesus went with Jairus.

This account of the day when a little girl died, was brought back to life by Jesus and was given something to eat by her overjoyed parents is many people's favourite Bible story. It's so gentle, so simply good, such an exquisite miracle.

What can we learn about good fathering from Jairus? Well, for a start, he values his daughter very highly, at a time when girls had very little social status. Then, he loves her enough to risk never seeing her alive again, leaving her side while she is dying and personally seeking help from a man for whom, until now, he has probably had little time. Not only that, but he is prepared to risk his reputation to save her life. Being in charge of the synagogue meant that he must have met many of Jesus' chief enemies, including Pharisees and priests. But right now, all that matters is his twelve-year-old daughter and, all dignity abandoned, he kneels in the street in front of a huge crowd and begs this unusual rabbi to come to his home in order to save her.

Even when some men arrive with the news that she is dead, he doesn't give up. He could have run home to join in the mourning, telling Jesus not to bother. He could have berated Jesus for taking too much time over some stupid woman who held him up for so long that the girl died before he could get to her (vv. 25–34). Instead, he accompanies Jesus back to the house, risks looking a total fool and allows him to lay hands on and speak into the ear of his dead child.

There are times when we are asked to sacrifice our carefully assembled principles, our sense of dignity and our own agendas and give our all for our children, simply because they need us.

....

Jesus 'made himself nothing, taking the very nature of a servant... he humbled himself and became obedient to death, even death on a cross!' (Philippians 2:7–8, NIV). Thank God for Jesus.

BP

Hope

God is always fair… God cannot tell lies! And so his promises and vows are two things that can never be changed. We have run to God for safety. Now his promises should greatly encourage us to take hold of the hope that is right in front of us… Hope reaches behind the curtain and into the most holy place.

Did you ever, as a child, feel ashamed of your father? I am in a huddle in the junior playground and we are discussing our fathers' jobs. 'My dad's a baker,' says one, extolling the joys of homemade bread and pink iced fairy cakes. 'My dad's a vet.' 'Mine's a policeman.' The list of exciting, fun and even dangerous occupations continues, each child basking in the group's appreciation of her good fortune in having such a father. 'Bridget, what does your dad do?' I look round the circle and want to die. The popularity stakes are high. 'Works in a bank,' I mumble, ashamed to admit that he has such a boring occupation. How incredibly silly of me—my poor hardworking father! Yet I can still tune into the hot misery of that day.

It's a feeling I've experienced a few times since, in fact—whenever natural disasters hit a region and are deemed an 'act of God'. 'Your God's useless,' I hear the media cry. 'How can a loving God let this happen?' I experience it when a friend asks me to explain some horrific vengeful act by God in the Old Testament, and when bad things happen to good people. I almost feel ashamed of my heavenly Father.

Wrestling with the 'why?' and the 'why didn't he?' will accompany many of us to the grave, but just as I can see now how stupid my childhood reactions were, so I hold on to the hope that reaches behind the curtain, and I maintain a belief that one day, in heaven, I will understand why things go so wrong and why my heavenly Father sometimes speaks, sometimes remains silent and sometimes seems to do nothing.

Lord, help us hang on to our flimsy faith until we can finally truly understand.

BP

Undeserved kindness

Your laws never leave my mind, and they make me much wiser than my enemies… I obey your word instead of following a way that leads to trouble… Your teachings are sweeter than honey. They give me understanding and make me hate all lies.

A friend of ours was sent away to boarding school when he was very young. Standing in the quadrangle, he fought back tears as his father bent to give him a hug before getting into the car that would carry him away for a whole term. 'This is an important piece of advice I'm going to give you,' said his dad, quietly. Patrick waited, imagining that his father was going to deliver a lecture about standing up for himself or telling the truth. 'Son, always be kind to the other boys.' This one piece of advice from a good father has informed and challenged the attitudes and actions of this person throughout his life.

The essence of the teachings of Jesus contains the same simple challenge. Love your neighbours as yourself. Forgive us our sins as we forgive others. Lay down your life for your friend.

Sometimes we struggle with the way our children interpret Christ's teaching as they grow up, especially if they have been encouraged to think for themselves. Many young adults cannot begin to understand how someone's sexual orientation can make them unacceptable to the church. Being kind and loving your neighbour must surely include tolerance and acceptance of difference. For some of our children, this goes as far as accepting that all religions are equal. Views such as these sometimes challenge and sometimes convince me, and sometimes leave me still believing they are misguided. However, I'm sure that the piece of parental advice I quoted earlier sums up the way of grace in the best possible way. Show to everyone you meet the undeserved kindness of our Father and leave him to sort out the rest.

....

The Bible repeatedly describes the Lord our God as 'slow to anger, abounding in love'. Invite God to fill you to overflowing with his love and grace, leaving judgment to him alone.

BP

Chosen children

The Law controlled us and kept us under its power until the time came when we would have faith... Children who are under age are no better off than slaves, even though everything their parents own will someday be theirs... That is how it was with us. We were like children ruled by the powers of the world... Now that we are his children, God has sent the Spirit of his Son into our hearts.

The Law's slaves, children ruled by the powers of the world, or God's children: which are we? If we have chosen to become God's children, then the external law is there to support us; but, because it is now written on our hearts, we have to take responsibility for our own attitudes and actions. We need to check our staple diet to see how much of the world media's junk food we have digested. We must keep an eye on the things that absorb most of our time. Are we slaves to work, the house, the children, the television, diets, even church activities? We need to become aware of our own inclinations and avoid situations that we know we are too weak to resist. We should listen to our conscience and make decisions in light of the fact that our Father in heaven can be hurt and his reputation damaged by what we, his children, do and say. In other words, we have to grow up.

But we also have access to a peace that the world cannot give, open arms to run back into, a Father who hears our sobbing and sees our efforts. Jesus said, 'When you pray, go into a room alone and close the door. Pray to your Father in private. He knows what is done in private, and he will reward you' (Matthew 6:6). He, like the very best human fathers (but, of course, even more so), knows the battles we fight as we try to be good and kind. He sees when we fail and when we try our best. He knows us through and through but still loves us. He is a Father who, in the words of the author Anne Lammot, 'loves us as we are and far too much to leave us as we are'.

....

Don't leave us as we are, dear Father. Help us to grow in your love.

                                                                    BP

Bonds of love

'My followers belong to you and I am praying for them… I am one with them and you are one with me, so that they may become completely one… Then the love that you have for me will become part of them, and I will be one with them.'

Often, Jesus took himself away from the crowd and from his disciples to pray alone, so that he could talk to his Father in private and receive strength and comfort. Yet here he prays aloud, clearly wanting his friends to hear exactly what he is saying. What comfort this prayer must have given them! But it's not just for them; it's for us as well: 'I am also praying for everyone else who will have faith because of what my followers will say about me' (v. 20).

God our Father has chosen us to be in his family, which means that we are special, whether we feel like it or not. All the wonderful stories, the miracles and the adventures came from him. Clearly it was not all going to end for the disciples when their beloved Jesus returned to his Father, or even when his followers came to the end of their ministry or their lives, and it is not going to end for us.

Do you enjoy being in airport arrival areas? I do. I am especially fascinated when planes arrive from the other side of the world and grandparents meet little ones for the first time, or when parents and children are reunited, sometimes after many years. The bonds of love have not been broken, and that is what Jesus is saying here. His followers, and that includes us, are still going to belong. We are one with Jesus, one with the Spirit and one with God the Father. Human families sometimes mess up big-time and people get hurt. Isn't it wonderful to know that our family in heaven will never bicker, and never abandon, despise or misunderstand any other person?

Take heart. That family is headed up by the Father who loves the followers of Jesus as much as they love and trust their Master.

....

We're on our way home, dear Father. Keep us safe until we get to you.

BP

What was your relationship like with your father? Where a father–child relationship is good, children like to please their father because they love him. A child might take up the same hobby as Dad, or follow the same sports team. Jesus learned his earthly father's trade as a carpenter but, by the time he was twelve years old, he already knew that his priority was to be in his heavenly Father's house, about his heavenly Father's business.

When he was alive, the Christian leader and teacher John Wimber encouraged people to continually ask, 'What is the Father doing?' Wimber saw many people healed as he asked that question, watching to see where God was already at work in people's lives and praying into those situations, asking God for miracles.

Over the next fortnight, Alie Stibbe will be considering 'Facing the second half of life' as she turns 50. You might have passed that milestone or it might still be some way off, but we can all use these two weeks at the midpoint of the year to take stock.

Ask yourself the question, 'What is the Father doing in my life and the lives of those around me? Am I focused on my heavenly Father's business, or am I doing my own thing? Am I living to please God or is my focus on pleasing others or only myself? Are there things God has called me to do, which I have been putting off? Are there people God has called me to pray for... tasks he has prompted me to do... gifts he has given me to use?'

Take time out to take stock.

Looking back to look forward

Remember the former things, those of long ago; I am God, and there is no other; I am God, and there is none like me. I make known the end from the beginning, from ancient times, what is still to come. I say: My purpose will stand, and I will do all that I please.

This year I will turn 50. It's not something a woman likes to admit, but there is no avoiding it. Rather like the years running up to my 40th birthday, the passing months have become a time to take stock. At that time, I identified three things I wanted to do but had not achieved: learn a language, learn a musical instrument and have a fourth child. All three have been achieved, and more, and now the pertinent question is 'What next?' This time, though, it's different. Before, there was more time ahead of me than behind me. Now the converse is true, and the way I spend the second half of life is a more serious matter than how I was to spend my fifth decade.

I have always found that an important part of planning my future is to remember God's faithfulness to me in the past. Taking time to chart my spiritual journey and the path along which I have been led always restores a long-term sense of perspective to my apparently capricious present circumstances. Remembering 'the former things' reminds me that God's goodness has followed me all the days of my life, even in dark and difficult circumstances. Life hasn't always worked out the way I have wanted, but I have come to learn that the Lord has his own purposes and he will do what he pleases. My job is to learn to align my will with his, to make the experience pleasurable. After a major upheaval in our personal circumstances, I am not sure of the path that lies ahead of me, but I am reassured to know that 'even to your old age and grey hairs I am he who will sustain you. I have made you and I will carry you' (v. 4).

....

Whatever your stage of life, take time to look back and be thankful for the Lord's faithfulness in all he has done for you over the months and years.

AS

Externals and peripherals

Remember your Creator in the days of your youth, before the days of trouble come and the years approach when you will say, 'I find no pleasure in them.'

I was out with my daughter recently when we heard a volley of wolf-whistles. I looked round in mock annoyance—only to realise that the whistles were aimed not at me but at my now grown-up and very beautiful daughter. At moments like that, it sinks in that your appearance is not all it once was, and that a great many middle-aged women are indeed 'invisible'. While there is great freedom in being able to get on with your life without worrying about who might be looking at you, there is more than a small degree of grief in coming to terms with the fact that your narrow waist and broad mind have begun to change places, and everything else is 'heading south'.

Rather than growing bitter that I am now upstaged by a daughter who could not zip up my wedding dress when she was eleven years old, I have decided on another tactic. The wife of noble character can 'laugh at the days to come' because 'she is clothed with strength and dignity' (Proverbs 31:25). This tells us that, ultimately, beauty is about our inner character. Character comes from the work of the Spirit within us and is not dependent on what we are wearing, our shape, or the absence of wrinkles. Coco Chanel said, 'Nature gives you the face you have at 20; it is up to you to merit the face you have at 50.' In my book, the face you have at 50 is a reflection of the work you have allowed the Lord to do in your heart since you were 20, not the amount of moisturiser you have used. The woman who has Christ shining through her eyes is the most beautiful of all, however old she may be.

....

'Charm is deceptive, and beauty is fleeting; but a woman who fears the Lord is to be praised' (Proverbs 31:30).

AS

A deeper wisdom

Blessed are those who find wisdom… Long life is in her right hand; in her left hand are riches and honour… She is a tree of life to those who embrace her; those who lay hold of her will be blessed.

When I was younger, I knew a Christian woman whom my children called 'the shiny lady'. She emanated a tangible sense of peace and calm. I remember thinking that when I 'grew up' (I was then 38!) I wanted to be like her. Now I am somewhat older, I realise that what I saw in that woman was the elusive and mysterious quality known as 'wisdom'.

We tend to think of wisdom as a gift of age, but it is by no means assured—there is such a thing as 'an old fool'. I certainly don't want to be one of those! I want to see the fruit of spiritual wisdom in my life. One way this can happen is through the gathered wealth of experience that life has thrown at us, especially if we have dealt with those troughs and peaks hand-in-hand with God and steeped in his word.

By my handling of the radical changes in my life in the last twelve months, I can tell that I do not yet have a level of spiritual wisdom akin to 'the shiny lady's'. I still allow myself to fret when my boat is rocked by the storms of life, and my new work situation has some-what knocked my self-confidence. Yet even these experiences can be grist to the mill if I step back from the whirl around me and allow the Lord time to make a pearl out of the sand I have let sneak into life's oyster shell. Like happiness, wisdom is a byproduct of a life spent hand-in-hand with God. We cannot rush it, only take one step at a time. In another ten years I hope I will be able to look back in won-der at what God has worked in my soul.

....

Lord, help me take time apart from the rush of the world to lay my experiences at your feet, so that I can learn the wisdom found in your heart.

AS

Passion and purpose

The righteous will flourish like a palm tree, they will grow like a cedar of Lebanon… They will still bear fruit in old age, they will stay fresh and green.

My husband has left his role in parish ministry to move from what he calls 'success' to 'significance'. He now heads up a charity that addresses the spiritual roots of fatherlessness in contemporary society. The whole of my life has once again shifted to fit in with his career move. In the process, I have achieved the dream of owning our own home—which I absolutely love—but I have lost all sense of direction in relation to my own career. 'You're moving from success to significance,' I wail, 'when I don't think I've even been successful! I haven't got much time left. What hope is there for me to catch up with you?'

As women age, the need to do something meaningful and important becomes increasingly urgent. I find I am no exception: I want to belong and make a significant contribution to something, somewhere, that matters to me. My husband tells me that first I have to identify my underlying passion, my life's script—or something like that. I am not sure I have one, except that I want to do whatever I do with excellence, and encourage other women to fulfil that same potential in their lives.

I know that my first task is to ditch the tendency to compare myself with others, especially my husband. We are not all cut out for such greatness. I have begun to understand that I can be a 'success' even in a low-key job and, perhaps, bring changes that make things work better in the future. Having reached that level of acceptance, I find that I am beginning to flourish after a few years of stagnation. I'm not quite a 'palm tree' yet, but it would be good to grow into a 'cedar of Lebanon'—something rooted and established.

....

Lord, never let me forget that if I acknowledge you in all my ways, you will make my paths straight (Proverbs 3:6).

AS

Friends for life

'But grant me this one request,' she said. 'Give me two months to roam the hills and weep with my friends, because I will never marry.'

The story of Jephthah the Gileadite's rash promise is one of the saddest in the Bible. Due to an ill-conceived vow, he ends up sacrificing his daughter because the Lord gives him victory over the Ammonites. I never cease to be astounded at the unnamed daughter's compliance in her father's foolishness—but in her request to her father is one of only two references to women's friendship that I can find in the Bible. The ill-fated girl asks for two months to weep and mourn with her friends; and in Luke 15:9 the woman who loses and finds a coin from her bridal headpiece calls her friends to come and share in her rejoicing.

Even in these two isolated references to women's friendship we can see that, from earliest times, women have turned to each other to make the good times better and the bad times bearable. I must admit, I am not a natural when it comes to making friends: I think I have been burnt too many times in 25 years of parish life. Yet, despite worrying about making myself vulnerable, I have determined to make an effort in the second half of life to be a friend and to make friends. Moreover, medical research tells us that people with 'close, non-toxic friends live longer than those who lack them' (Pamela Blair, *The Next Fifty Years*). I'm up for that!

Facing up to 50 and starting out on a new phase of life is a great time to figure out who are the friends you want to keep for the next stage, and to be on the lookout for new ones. But let's remember that the most important thing is what we contribute to a relationship, not what we think we can get out of it.

Lord, help us get over the isolation that we grow accustomed to in today's world, and draw us into relationship with others.

AS

Money or nothing?

Our people must learn to devote themselves to doing what is good, in order that they may provide for daily necessities and not live unproductive lives.

Material provision can be a big consideration in the second half of life. In biblical times, women had few rights when it came to property and possessions; becoming a widow was akin to losing everything if you did not have a family to look after you. Times have changed and there is now no excuse for a woman not to familiarise herself with the way the household finances work—if she is not the one in charge of them already! It is a salutary fact that 85 per cent of women out-live their husbands, and the weeks after bereavement are not the best time to be getting your head around bills and standing orders. If you don't believe me, and the bills are in someone else's name at your home address, try talking to one of your household service providers: they won't speak to you at all, due to data protection—even if you say that the account holder is your husband and he's dead! If you trust your husband not to do a runner, it may be an idea to have all bills put in both your names—or ask him to nominate you as having authority to speak on his behalf. I have had to do this because my husband is abroad so often that he can't deal with his own credit cards all of the time. It's a good job he trusts me: I could have gone on a shopping spree years ago!

Retirement was not a social option in biblical times, either: you worked yourself into the grave, as our generation will probably have to do. None of us knows what the future holds, but it may be wise to get our heads out of the sand and think ahead while there is still time left to put a godly action plan in place (Proverbs 30:24–25).

....

'I was young and now I am old, yet I have never seen the righteous forsaken or their children begging bread' (Psalm 37:25).

AS

Leaving a legacy

Likewise, teach the older women to be reverent in the way they live, not to be slanderers or addicted to much wine, but to teach what is good.

I don't think I am going to be in a position to leave our four children much in a material sense, but 'leaving a legacy' need not mean that your will describes a copious list of goodies to be distributed among your family (probably leading to more dissention than rejoicing). Legacy is more about how you want to be remembered. Of course, not all of us are going down in the history books—the memory of us may not outlive our grandchildren (Ecclesiastes 9:5)—but we can hand down our stories, our experiences and, we hope, the example of a gracious and generous character that will mould the next generation.

I was talking to my daughter and her friend early this morning. He volunteered that his mother was a Catholic. 'You're nothing, aren't you, Mum?' said my daughter. 'I'm a Christian,' I retorted quickly, thinking that she meant I had no faith at all (everything has been up for grabs in the last year since leaving parish life), but then slowly realising, with some relief, that she meant I was not affiliated to any particular denomination.

Our children, our daughters, pick up more about us and from us than we realise. Even when we think they are grown up and deciding for themselves, they are still looking to us for silent guidance in the way we live our lives and relate to others. I have suddenly figured out that the empty nest is not an excuse to relax our standards, even if we are trying to figure out our values and beliefs in relation to our own changing lives. The next generation needs to see some consistency: we need to teach what is good in what we say and in what we do. So from now on I'd better have my midlife crisis in private!

....

'Search me, O God, and know my heart; test me and know my anxious thoughts. See if there is any offensive way in me, and lead me in the way everlasting' (Psalm 139:23–24).

AS

A 'mid-life crisis' and dramatic change of circumstances prompted Alie Stibbe to take stock of life. A different but equally dramatic crisis prompted a complete turn-around for Rosemary Green, who takes us through the next week's devotions.

Life's crises can disable us or enable us to change. Some of the most dramatic transformations for good take place in people's inner lives when possessions, relationships, positions of responsibility and self-respect are all stripped away.

Looking back over your own life, have there been many crises? How have you reacted? How have these difficult times been a catalyst for change? Have there been lessons to learn? How have you grown as a result of life's challenges?

For centuries, people have used pilgrimage or retreats to draw closer to God, away from other distractions. In the TV documentary series *The Big Silence*, participants were taken on a silent retreat, and even the atheists among the group were surprised at the profound impact the experiment had on them.

Has your life become cluttered? Could you find new clarity or direction from a period of time spent living with less? Often we need to retreat to advance into new areas; we can learn to appreciate what we have when we learn to do without. Sometimes we need to go back to basics.

Rosemary Green's focus is on one of life's basics—meals—which Jesus put at the very centre of the Christian faith. The Passover meal had been at the centre of Jewish life; Jesus transformed it by his death and resurrection, encouraging us to remember him regularly as we share a meal together.

Over this next week, make each meal special, thanking God for his provision for you and asking God to feed your Spirit in new ways as you look for fresh opportunities to share his love with those around you.

Hospitality with a purpose

'Follow me,' Jesus said to him, and Levi got up, left everything
and followed him. Then Levi held a great banquet for Jesus at his
house, and a large crowd of tax collectors and others were eating
with them.

I look back at a point when my 'churchianity' changed into Christianity. At the time, it seemed like a crisis weekend (a good kind of crisis),
but later I saw how God had been preparing me, particularly over the
previous year. Was it something like that with Levi? From this incident, it looks as if Jesus suddenly appeared in front of him and—hey
presto!—there was an instant response to the call to follow him. But
before this I guess that the taxman, sitting in his booth, had overheard
discussion about this new teacher and miracle worker, and had been
in the crowd, listening and watching, before their face-to-face meeting. It is good to look back and see how God prepared each of us to
follow him. Each of us has a story to tell; each story is valid, however
gentle or spectacular.

What interests me most today, though, is what Levi did next. He
held a party for all his old friends, with Jesus as the guest of honour.
He was declaring that he was now a Jesus follower, and he wanted
his friends to meet him too—these friends who (as the Pharisees complained) were outside the respectable religious circles. It sounds like
a big party! That implies a large house, owned by a rich man. But we
do not have to live in a big home to be able to use it for the Lord. I
know a single mother who supplements her income by home sales of
cosmetics. She has gradually developed relationships with her cus-
tomers, offering support, lifts to hospital and prayer in times of crisis.
Now she plans a tea party (maximum eight people to squeeze into
her living-room) to discuss the question 'Does God answer prayer?'
I call it a 'Matthew party'.

....

*Lord, please show me how I can
use my home to help my friends
to know you.*

See Acts 10:24–48 to find
another man who invited friends
and relations into his home to
hear the gospel.

RG

75

Dangerous promises!

*On his birthday Herod gave a banquet… When the daughter of
Herodias came in and danced, she pleased Herod and his dinner
guests. The king said to the girl, 'Ask me for anything you want,
and I'll give it to you… up to half my kingdom.'*

Herod Antipas and his family were exceptionally nasty pieces of
work. His father, Herod the Great, had ordered the murder of the
young boys in Bethlehem, and the family's relationships were tangled.
Herodias, a granddaughter of Herod the Great, had first married her
uncle Philip, then divorced him in favour of his half-brother Antipas
(also her uncle, also divorced). It was this second marriage that John
the Baptist denounced as illegal. A furious Herodias wanted John exe-
cuted, but Herod respected him and refused his wife's demands.

Then came his lavish birthday party in Tiberias, on the shores of
Lake Galilee. Well dined and wined, the guests enjoyed Salome's
dancing. They all heard Herod's spontaneous, generous promise: 'Ask
me for anything you want.' Her request for John's head put him in
a dilemma, but his fear of losing face with his guests overcame his
conscience at executing a man whom he recognised as 'righteous
and holy' (v. 20). What a contrast with John himself, who, for conscience's sake, was unafraid to rebuke the king! So a servant made
the 200-mile round trip to Machaerus, the fortress near the Dead Sea
where John was imprisoned, and returned with the prisoner's head.

There are many lessons we could draw from this unhappy story.
Among them is the danger of making rash promises. We easily make
good promises with the best of intentions, but don't carry them
through when forgetfulness or lack of resources intervene. At other
times there are rash spur-of-the-moment promises, made without
thinking of the possible implications. Promises are meant to be kept,
so make them thoughtfully.

....

*Lord, in my promises, may I look
before I leap.*

Read a tragic story of a rash
promise in Judges 11:29–35.

                                                                            RG

Food in the desert

When Jesus looked up and saw a great crowd coming towards him, he said to Philip, 'Where shall we buy bread for these people to eat?' ... Jesus then took the loaves, gave thanks, and distributed to those who were seated as much as they wanted.

Several years ago, my husband and I were privileged to be in the Solomon Islands. One Sunday morning he preached in a crowded cathedral—the overflow no problem, as the building had a roof but no walls. Afterwards, over 2000 of us sat on the grass alongside long rows of banana leaves, which served as both tables and plates. It was a memorable experience that brought alive today's reading.

This is the only miracle that is recorded in all four Gospels. The accounts share a common outline but include different details. All agree that twelve basketsful of leftovers were collected—amazingly, more than they started with. Matthew 14:21 makes it clear that far more than 5000 were fed: they didn't count the women and children.

Jesus had taken his disciples away because they all needed time to retreat—Jesus grieving over the death of his cousin John (Luke 9:10), the Twelve needing rest after a mission trip (Mark 6:30–31). John tells us about Andrew finding the boy with his picnic. (Whenever we meet Andrew in John's Gospel, he is introducing someone to Jesus.) Matthew and Mark tell us of Jesus' compassion for the crowd, Luke that he welcomed them. These different facets of the story are not contradictory but together they build up a complete picture of the scene.

Like the other miracles, though, this is not just a story about Jesus and his supernatural powers. The Jews believed that food in the desert was a mark of the messianic age. So, by feeding the crowd in this way, Jesus was making a covert statement about his claim to be the Messiah—and this gives significance to John 6:25–59, about Jesus as the bread of life.

....

Thank you, Lord, that every person matters to you, for times of quiet retreat, for your understanding when we grieve, for your compassion for the needy, and for your amazing power. Above all, thank you that you came as Messiah and Saviour.

RG

Forgiveness and love

'Do you see this woman? I entered your house; you gave me no water for my feet, but she has bathed my feet with her tears... Therefore, I tell you, her sins, which were many, have been forgiven; hence she has shown great love.'

This story is full of surprises. Surprise number 1: Jesus was invited to a meal in a Pharisee's house. That didn't happen often. Surprise number 2: the host forgot the common courtesy of ensuring that his guests' sandal-covered feet were washed after walking on dusty roads. Surprise number 3: a known prostitute gained entrance to this respectable house. Surprise number 4: she went where the guests were reclining to eat, as was the contemporary custom. She stood behind Jesus, weeping profusely. Her tears dripped on to his feet before she wiped them with her long hair, kissed them and poured out her ointment. Surprise number 5: Jesus didn't rebuke her! 'If this man were a prophet, he would have known...' (v. 39). Yes, Jesus did know the woman, but he also knew Simon's silent thoughts, and addressed him with a parable, a question and a rebuke.

The biggest surprise of all, though, came when Jesus approved the woman's actions. He saw her lavish generosity; he also saw her love for him, born of his lavish forgiveness for her sin. This challenges me. God wants us to be sure—sure at gut level as well as in our heads—that he forgives us. I am certain that he has forgiven me for many things: he has forgiven my burst of temper over a young woman, which had huge repercussions for our church; he has forgiven me for breaking my mother-in-law's fragile ribs in a strong hug born of a complex mixture of compassion and anger, and for a friendship that started well but became disproportionately important. But does my love for Jesus match the generosity of his forgiveness? My many sins have been forgiven, but do I love him too little?

....

Meditate on Isaiah 43:25, the verse that convinced me that God really does forgive and forget.

RG

A meal to remember

Whenever you eat this bread and drink this cup, you proclaim the Lord's death until he comes. Therefore, whoever eats the bread or drinks the cup of the Lord in an unworthy manner will be guilty of sinning against the body and blood of the Lord.

Last Maundy Thursday evening, we changed our usual practice of holding a Communion service in church. Instead, a fish and chips supper in the church hall was followed by remembering Jesus with his disciples in the upper room. As 40 of us passed round the bread and the wine, it seemed that our shared meal was more like the way the early Christians kept the Lord's supper than our usual Communion service. Less dignified, maybe, but the warmth of our fellowship was enhanced by the simple meal and the informality of the worship.

The situation in Corinth, however, was spoilt by division (v. 18) and by the selfishness and greed of many of the Christians, who didn't respect their fellow believers. They would meet in the large home of one of the richer Christians. Those who arrived first—the well-off and well-fed—didn't wait for the workers, the slaves. They were oblivious to the example Jesus set when he washed his disciples' feet. Paul, after reminding them of how this meal started, gave them a solemn warning about the sin involved when they behaved in such an unChrist-like way.

When I come to a Communion service (wherever and however it is held), I find it helpful to remember six directions in which to look. We look *in*, in self-examination and repentance (vv. 27–28). We look *round* in love to the community of believers (v. 33). We look *back*, remembering Jesus and his death (vv. 23–25). We look *up* to the Lord who feeds us and judges us (v. 32). We look *out* to proclaim Jesus to those who do not know him, and we look *forward* to his return (v. 26).

Lord Jesus, thank you for this special meal you gave us. I pray that it may remain fresh and alive to me every time I take part.

RG

A walk to remember

When he was at the table with them, he took bread, gave thanks, broke it and began to give it to them. Then their eyes were opened and they recognised him.

It had been a rollercoaster weekend. Cleopas and his companion (perhaps his wife) had plenty to think about as they trudged home from Jerusalem that afternoon. Their high hopes that Jesus would be their nation's saviour had been dashed by his crucifixion. The sabbath had been a day of utter gloom for his followers. Then came startling news from the women, after their early morning visit to the tomb: 'We saw two angels who told us he has risen!' An incredible story, confirmed by Peter and John, who saw the empty tomb and the shroud. The couple's thoughts and emotions were churning as they walked and talked. Do you remember times when shattering events have left your mind and stomach both turning somersaults?

Then the apparent stranger caught up with them. 'What are you discussing?' His simple, open question led into the most exciting Bible lesson of their lives, covering so much of the scripture that they knew—yet didn't really know. Whenever we read the Bible (Old and New Testament alike), we can pray that the Spirit will enlighten our minds and our souls, so that we expect our hearts to 'burn within us' (v. 32). Our Bible reading too easily becomes a dull, boring routine instead of the enlivening experience that God wants it to be.

Even then, the couple didn't recognise their teacher-companion. In natural concern for a late traveller, they invited him into their home. They must have been momentarily surprised when their guest took the host's role at the simple meal, gave thanks and broke the bread. Then they recognised him! There was something in that prayer and in that act that opened their eyes. They were so excited that they hurried back seven miles in the dark to tell their friends.

....

Consider three vital elements in getting to know Jesus better: expectant Bible reading, sharing in the Communion service, and telling others about the risen Jesus.

RG

A special breakfast

'Simon son of John, do you truly love me…?' 'Yes, Lord,' he said, 'you know that I love you.' Jesus said, 'Feed my lambs.'

On his seventh birthday, our grandson chose a fishing trip for the family outing. Three rods were set up on the lake shore and we waited for a bite. We played with a football to keep warm. No fish. The boys dug some clay. Still no fish. We ate our picnic lunch. Finally the rods moved and three fine trout were landed.

Those two hours of waiting for the fish seemed a lo-o-o-ong time. For the seven disciples in today's reading, the night must have seemed endless. Then, in the early morning, a stranger called out, 'Throw the net out again!' They might have grumbled ('What does he know about fishing?') but they obeyed the authoritative, encouraging voice. Immediately the net was full, too heavy to pull into the boat. The insightful John recognised Jesus; the impetuous Peter jumped into the shallow water to wade to him, while the rest pulled in the boat and its load.

The fire was already lit and breakfast was ready. After breakfast the others carefully counted the fish (as fishermen would!) while Peter had a private conversation with Jesus. 'Do you really love me, Simon?' The Greek word Jesus used is a strong one: 'Are you devoted to me? More than these others are?' Peter's reply was weaker: 'Yes, Lord, you know I am fond of you.' Was he still ashamed of his three-fold denial of Jesus? Three times the question was asked; three times Peter affirmed his love for Jesus; three times Jesus called him to be a shepherd of the flock. Jesus wanted Peter to be sure that he was forgiven, loved, needed. That was reassurance indeed.

I doubt if Peter paid much attention to Jesus' warning about the dependency of old age (v. 18); John, writing his Gospel after Peter's death, understood it better.

....

Lord Jesus, thank you that you know me, love me, forgive me and want to use me.

See Zechariah 3:1–7 for a graphic picture of a spiritual leader forgiven and recommissioned for service.

RG

Anne Le Tissier writes:

I wonder what springs to mind when we hear or read about 'the fear of God'? Perhaps we picture Mount Sinai, obscured in smoke, fortified by thunder, its skies scorched with lightning as the cowering Israelites tremble with terror beneath God's holy presence; or a black-clad preacher thumping the lectern, commanding his hearers to fear God—his wrath, hell and damnation.

We might imagine Abram prostrate, Moses removing his sandals, or a priest genuflecting as he passes by the altar. We may even recall a cautionary Bible text inscribed above a church doorway, warning those who enter that they walk on holy ground. Or perhaps we think of Dickensian schoolmasters enforcing their idea of God-fearing obedience by shaming, starving or beating a frightened child; Pharisees making great displays of supposed pious behaviour; austere religious ascetics, or uneasy men looking uncomfortable in buttoned-up three-piece suits on a rare but obligatory attendance at church.

Is this what it means to fear God: an outward display of obeisance, discomfort, terror or 'holy' behaviour? Should we too be trembling in our shoes when we think of and speak with God? Is such a response confined to the Old Testament, before Jesus repeatedly said, 'Do not be afraid'? Or might it suggest something else?

It is true that, without a fear of God, we are more prone to compromise the godly lifestyles that he has called us to live, but there is more to this topic than religious piety. In fact, as we take time to renew our appreciation of the fear of God and consider its implications, I trust that he will continue to hone our lives, edify our faith and put the world back into the right perspective. He will release us from all other fears—real or perceived, blatant or subtle—which hinder or goad us, keep us awake at night or even make us unwell. In turn, I believe we may reap the many blessings that God has promised to those who fear him. 'Fear God and keep his commandments, for this is the duty of every human being' (Ecclesiastes 12:13).

What is 'the fear of God'?

God is love. Those who live in love live in God, and God in them. In this way, love is made complete among us so that we will have confidence on the day of judgment... Perfect love drives out fear, because fear has to do with punishment.

'Fear' may have negative connotations. My dictionary, for instance, begins by defining fear as 'a feeling of distress, apprehension or alarm caused by impending danger'. That definition aptly describes the Israelites trembling at the foot of Mount Sinai, distressed by God's powerful presence, against which they had no defence (Exodus 19:16–19).

Perhaps their experience foreshadows God's final judgment on those who have not been reconciled to him through believing and surrendering to Christ—the fear of God's power and anger that some may even feel already, and of his punishment in this life or the next. Sadly, such feelings arise where knowledge or experience of God's love is lacking, overshadowed by a message of guilt and condemnation and an unbalanced portrayal of his character.

My dictionary gives another definition, though, describing fear as 'divine awe and reverence'. This highlights a feeling of profound respect for God, and an outward manifestation of that feeling.

Abram wasn't displaying terror when he prostrated himself before God in Genesis 17:3 and 17. Overwhelmed by God's love, power, purpose and promise, it didn't feel right to remain standing—so he fell face down to the ground. It was the natural, physical outworking of the feeling he held in his heart—an attitude of reverence and awe, with overwhelming wonder, admiration and respect for God.

I trust we've all experienced God's forgiveness through belief in Christ. But even in this profound relationship of perfect love, there is still a place for fear—in the sense of reverent awe—for prostrating our hearts and minds and, at times, our bodies, in honour of who God is.

....

Lord, your love has certainly melted my heart and I delight to praise you. Indeed, you are awesome, and I bow before your majesty.

ALeT

The fear of God for today

Therefore, since we are receiving a kingdom that cannot be shaken, let us be thankful, and so worship God acceptably with reverence and awe, for our 'God is a consuming fire'.

I've been saddened to read one or two contemporary authors who describe our faithful, loving, compassionate God as tyrannical and masochistic, to name just two of their mistaken perceptions that reveal a flawed understanding and warped interpretation of scripture.

The Old Testament God of rules and regulations, whose wrath was poured out on disobedient people, was and is no different from the God of grace and unconditional love revealed in his Son, Jesus. God is unchangeable—permanent in character, purpose and being. Through Christ, the covenant has changed from old to new, but God has not changed and is still to be feared and revered.

In fact, it might be said that we have a greater responsibility to uphold our fear of God because Christ has revealed him personally to our hearts through the Holy Spirit (v. 25). That is why, as we await the final consummation of God's eternal kingdom, we are to worship and serve God 'with reverence and awe' (v. 28).

'My dear friends,' Paul wrote, 'continue to work out your salvation with fear and trembling, for it is God who works in you to will and to act according to his good purpose' (Philippians 2:12–13). We, his created people, worship the same almighty, awesome, sovereign God of the patriarchs. Consequently, we continue to recognise and respect our humble status in relation to him. Furthermore, if we have acknowledged Jesus as Lord, we are under an obligation to obey him, demonstrating—not earning—our new life in Christ. And we do this 'with fear and trembling', in ways that revere and honour God. We are spurred on by a passionate desire not to grieve but to please and delight the one we love, who loves us with an everlasting love.

Do we worship God only for his love, goodness, faithfulness, holiness, power and forgiveness, or also for his justice, discipline and righteous anger?

ALeT

Fear manifested in obedience

And now… what does the Lord your God ask of you but to fear the Lord your God, to walk in all his ways, to love him, to serve the Lord your God with all your heart and with all your soul, and to observe the Lord's commands and decrees…?

I recently backed the car into a bollard at the rear of a parking space. I felt sick! It was one of those, 'If I only I could turn the clock back' moments. Of course I didn't do it intentionally, but it was a careless mistake that cracked the bumper and would be costly to repair. My husband is a loving, patient and forgiving man, but that didn't stop me fretting all day about telling him, or protect me from panicky twinges when I heard his key unlocking the front door.

I make many careless but unintentional mistakes in other ways, too—when I inadvertently judge or criticise someone, snap an irritated response, or waste time on irrelevancies instead of prioritising God's kingdom. But I don't fear admitting them because God is infinitely more loving, patient and forgiving even than my husband. The trouble is, I can be tempted to take God's perfect grace for granted.

Being careless, or perhaps even wilfully rebellious at times, with the life God has asked us to live suggests a shallow appreciation for his love and forgiveness, which saddens him. Furthermore, we reap what we sow: our actions may abuse his practical provision, misuse our physical body, or misrepresent his character and dishonour his reputation. All of these actions have potential consequences.

To fear God through obedient living is not an attempt to earn his favour, for God cannot be bribed (v. 17), but it does confirm our respect for who he is and what he has done. Indeed, if we *say* that we love him, it will be proved by our actions (John 14:23).

'Through the fear of the Lord evil is avoided' (Proverbs 16:6b). Do we exhibit a fear of God through obedient lives?

....

'Who can discern their errors? Forgive my hidden faults. Keep your servant also from wilful sins; may they not rule over me'
(Psalm 19:12–13).

ALeT

Fear for God's reputation—or mine?

'Who are you that you fear mere mortals… who are but grass, that you forget the Lord your Maker…?' … To fear anyone will prove to be a snare, but whoever trusts in the Lord is kept safe.

I was in the library recently, trying to press on with some research, when my attention was distracted by some students sharing my table. A young woman was talking about a chap she'd befriended, who she admitted might appear a bit 'odd'. She spoke warmly of his qualities but her friends, sadly, thought otherwise when he later popped by to say 'hello'. No sooner had he left than they mocked his educated accent, mimicked his lilting gait and scorned his fashion sense. She tried defending him but gave up when she too began to appear 'uncool' and was drawn into the same disparagement.

We call it peer pressure and, as adults, we're by no means immune. Our behaviour, our activities and the degree to which we share our faith may be driven by a concern to be liked, admired or approved by other people, even if our actions compromise or ignore God's ways. But when we fear what others think about us more than we fear what God thinks, our thoughts and emotions will be easily ensnared, discouraged and abused by the worldly ideals to which we aspire. How that saddens our Father's heart as he waits for us to run back into his arms; the place of freedom and unconditional love!

To fear what God thinks of us more than what others think is fundamental to a healthy sense of self-worth and contentment. Worldly pressures to conform may promise respect, popularity, admiration or success but do little more than attack, confuse and ultimately damage our innate sense of value as God's unique, loving handiwork.

Furthermore, to fear what people think about our faith and, therefore, not to share it may result in their eternal damnation. I wonder how often we consider what God thinks about that.

....

'Am I now trying to win human approval, or God's approval? … If I were still trying to please people, I would not be a servant of Christ' (Galatians 1:10).

ALeT

Fearing God's will

The Lord said to Moses, 'How long will these people treat me with contempt? How long will they refuse to believe in me, in spite of all the miraculous signs I have performed among them?'

I still grapple with the mysteries of creation and Old Testament culture, but I believe in the revelation of almighty God to an ancient people. I also believe wholeheartedly in the life, work, resurrection and saving power of Jesus Christ. I certainly wouldn't be walking the path I do now if I didn't have that faith. But perhaps, like the Hebrews, I limit God's potential in and through me, by failing to live by my beliefs—hesitating to put them into action when he asks me to step outside the boundaries of my understanding or capability.

The Hebrews marvelled at God's power revealed through the plagues, the Red Sea deliverance, provision of water from a rock, manna and quail, the glory of his presence in the pillars of cloud and fire, and the lightning and smoke of Mount Sinai. And yet, despite their first-hand experience, only two out of twelve leaders trusted God to equip them to take his promised land. It's a tragic story—in fact, terrifying, when we consider the repercussions of their hesitancy to continue in God's will, all because they were afraid of what their finite minds could understand and what their physical eyes perceived.

Perhaps God would ask of us, 'Do you want to experience the promised blessings and spiritual power of walking in my will? If so, do you fear me more than your own abilities and understanding, or those that you perceive in others?' Maybe we've been discouraged by problems and are wary of the powerful obstacles that seem to block the path of God's will. Or perhaps we've grown too content with life 'on the wrong side of the Jordan'. Either way, if such an attitude relays a message that we hold God's power in contempt, then join me in the following prayer.

....

Lord, I want to live in the fullness of the 'promised land' blessings— the life you intended for me to live. In faith I will take hold of it.

ALeT

Fear of God's jealousy

You shall have no other gods before me. You shall not make for yourself an idol in the form of anything… You shall not bow down to them or worship them; for I, the Lord your God, am a jealous God.

It's funny how we won't tolerate being two-timed, yet some people reject our faith on the basis that God's expectations, and discipline where necessary, are too harsh. But these words were not spoken by a tyrant; they were born out of love.

God is jealous because he loves us. Who isn't jealous for the love of the one they love? And yet, even Christians may find it hard to relate to these ancient demands. After all, we don't worship golden calves, Asherah poles or miniature or life-sized statues—at least, I hope not! But the consequence of such thinking may compromise our appreciation of God's jealousy and our response to it.

God hasn't changed. In James 4:5, we read, 'The spirit he caused to live in us envies intensely.' God is love—love that melts the hardest of hearts and cares for us unconditionally—but he is also a jealous God. Do we fear arousing that jealousy, or do we risk the discipline needed to bring us back into the life he intended, one filled to full measure with himself?

God longs to be our first love (Revelation 2:4). Is he? Or is something or someone else vying for our attention, stealing our time and passionate pursuit, so breaking our Father's heart? Who or what do we truly long for? God—or the next promotion, a husband, more money or a size 12 figure? Who or what do we think about most? God— or the next thing we want to buy, our children, worries, dreams or goals? Who or what fills up our prayer time? Expressions of our love for God—or making requests of him? To whom or what do we give our best efforts, our time, resources and talents? God—or our reputation, the pursuit of success, our hobbies, the house or our wardrobe?

....

Lord, I am mindful of .... vying for my time, heart and attention, yet nothing really compares to you. Earth has nothing I could desire besides you. I love you.

ALeT

Fearing God or this fallen world

God is our refuge and strength, an ever-present help in trouble.
Therefore we will not fear, though the earth give way and the
mountains fall into the heart of the sea, though its waters roar and
foam and the mountains quake with their surging.

Some of us may have fallen prey to certain 'worldly' fears. They are
very real to us and although we know that our fear of God should
allay such concerns, we've allowed them too great a hold on our
heart, will and emotions. We may suffer a debilitating fear in crowds
or in the dark, on planes or trains, being alone or in the company of
spiders or dogs. We may fear the potential effects of fire, theft or flood
should they visit our home. Or perhaps we suffer with an eating dis-
order and fear the reading on the bathroom scales, or with an alcohol
addiction and fear the consequence of someone finding out.

We may fear for our safety with terrorist threats, or the potential
effects of global warming. Perhaps we suffer an intimidating fear in
the company of intellectual, experienced or capable people, or fear
what people think if we pray out loud in a group.

God cares deeply that we would revere him and so be free from
these fears that distract our attention, sap our energy, consume our
thoughts, keep us awake at night, limit our potential or hinder our
social life. As we uphold our fear of God by taking regular time to
consider and acknowledge his character, power, faithfulness, purpose, love and so on, it leads us into a place where we can 'rest
content, untouched by trouble' (Proverbs 19:23).

It's not that all our problems will disappear, but, when we have
a right concept of who God is and revere him accordingly, those
troubles and anxieties prove powerless in their attempt to disrupt the
quality of rest and security that we have in God, and the blessings
and power we experience in a relationship of utmost trust.

....

*'Be still, and know that I am God' (Psalm 46:10). Still your heart,
mind and emotions; feed on his word, reflect in prayer, and know
your awesome God.*

ALeT

Fear of persecution

'Do not be afraid of those who kill the body but cannot kill the soul. Rather, be afraid of the One who can destroy both soul and body in hell.'

Although I've experienced ridicule and mild rejection from loved ones for my Christian beliefs, I've yet to encounter physical violence, imprisonment, the withdrawal of necessary care and provisions, and the threat of death that thousands experience daily.

Jesus, however, was hated from the moment he was born—perceived as being a threat to Herod's kingship (Matthew 2:3). His presence later threatened the authority of religious and political leaders, who subsequently tortured this humblest of men with the cruellest of deaths. But Jesus countered such oppression through miraculous intervention (Matthew 2:13), and by hiding himself or avoiding certain places where necessary (John 8:59; 11:54). When he knew his time was drawing to a close, he agonised in Gethsemane, passionately expressing his fears but humbly and sincerely surrendering to God's purpose (Mark 14:34–36). Jesus feared the consequence of living outside God's will far more than he feared what humans could do to him, and so he remained obedient to his Father, even to death.

Our times are also in God's hands, not the hands of our enemies (Psalm 31:15; John 8:20). God will continue to safeguard us, lead us and, where necessary, intervene, while we remain faithful to his name and his purpose. Furthermore, we need not worry about what to say if we are brought up before the authorities, for he assures us that the Spirit will speak through us (Matthew 10:19–20).

This is why we must continue to nurture our fear of God, which will keep us standing firm when faced with opposition, be it mild or severe. So, 'Do not be terrified by them, for the Lord your God, who is among you, is a great and awesome God' (Deuteronomy 7:21).

....

Father, hear and answer the cry of your persecuted people and meet their needs. Comfort their hearts, strengthen their minds and wills, and guard them from the evil one.

ALeT

Fear revealed in relationships

'Oh, that their hearts would be inclined to fear me and keep all my commands always, so that it might go well with them and their children for ever!'

The Ten Commandments—principles that God expected his people to adhere to and live by—include four that concern our relationship with God and six concerning our relationships with one another.

Ironically, the people who see me at my worst are my nearest and dearest. They encounter the aftermath of my stressful day; they are the unfortunate recipients of my overtired irritability, and the innocent party cut by my snappy retorts when I'm plain fed up. But showing respect for the elderly, valuing foreigners, supporting labourers, widows and orphans, obeying our employers, loving our unbelieving husbands, and generally encouraging, submitting to and showing respect to *everyone* are just a few examples of how our relationships may demonstrate our fear of the Lord.

We cannot say that we love and honour God unless we love and honour one another. We are, after all, his creations—uniquely made, loved and chosen. So, today, let's consider our relationships with spouse, parents, children, friends, church family, colleagues, occasional acquaintances, strangers in the street, and even people whom we've never met who might benefit from our prayers or practical support.

Is our love for each other influenced by the extent to which we personally relate to someone, by how well they treat us, how they behave, their nationality, upbringing, accent and so on? Or do we show unconditional love for all people, arising from our fear of God in obedience to his command to 'love one another' just as he loves us (John 15:12)?

....

Failing to offer anyone compassion, mercy, love or provision scorns rather than reveres their Maker. 'Do to others as you would have them do to you' (Luke 6:31).

ALeT

The fear of God in prayer

Then Joshua fell face down to the ground in reverence, and asked him, 'What message does my Lord have for his servant?' The commander of the Lord's army replied, 'Take off your sandals, for the place where you are standing is holy.' And Joshua did so.

I enjoy lateral thinking puzzles, forcing my mind to think 'outside the box' of logical explanations. I also need to do this in my consideration of God if I am to fear him as he deserves. 'Putting God in a box' is a familiar expression, suggesting a tendency to limit our appreciation of who he is and what he can do. We may dilute our fear of God by trying to understand him with the limited capacity of our human experience. Or perhaps we restrict our faith in his power because we expect him to work in ways that we want or can anticipate.

It feels safe and secure to think we can somehow 'manage' God. Perhaps we see prayer as a means to 'control' him, dictating to him how *we* think he should act in response to our need or our understanding of a situation. Maybe we subconsciously believe we can manipulate his attributes for our benefit or in line with our own opinions about life, faith and what is right or just.

Joshua was no different. On his approach to Jericho, he perceived two sides of a battle and wanted to know if God was on his side. Instead, he was taught to take off his sandals and get himself on God's side. In so doing, he was reminded that revering God meant honouring his presence, accepting his ways and obeying his instruction without further question.

Jesus 'offered up prayers and petitions and he was heard because of his reverent submission' (Hebrews 5:7). Do we revere God through our prayers? His thoughts and ways are, after all, far higher than ours (Isaiah 55:8–9). Before we're tempted to tell him what to do, let's learn to pause and praise, then discern his purpose in prayer.

....

Lord, may your will be done in my life and this world, rather than my own.

What can you learn from Jesus' prayer in Matthew 26:39?

ALeT

Fear for God's temple

Do not trust in deceptive words and say, 'This is the temple of the Lord, the temple of the Lord, the temple of the Lord!' … Will you… say, 'We are safe'—safe to do all these detestable things? Has this house, which bears my Name, become a den of robbers to you?

During a mission trip to India, I was amazed to see how readily certain Hindus would receive Christ. The problem was that they would only accept him as one of hundreds of gods. Similarly, I wonder if we sometimes seek to cover all our bases. Do we 'fear' feeling hurt, empty, confused, vulnerable, sad and so on, but rather than waiting on God's presence to fill our emotional void, seek out a temporary quick-fix—excess food, alcohol or inappropriate sex, for example?

'Do you not know that your bodies are temples of the Holy Spirit? … Therefore honour God with your body' (1 Corinthians 6:19–20). The Israelites compromised God's presence in his temple, but now that we are that temple, I wonder if we do, too? Have we also grown so accustomed to the presence of God with us that we've compromised our reverence for his house? Do we give a public appearance of reverent worship but, in the lone company of our Father, fail to uphold our godly fear by disregarding his dwelling?

If we truly revere the Lord, we shall also revere the upkeep and use of his 'home'. God ordained feasts for his people and Jesus turned water into wine. He delights in our enjoyment of physical pleasures, but he also denounces excessive indulgence. Food is necessary for survival but greed is condemned as idolatry (Colossians 3:5). Alcohol has been drunk since Noah's day, but drunkenness belongs to the sinful nature (Galatians 5:21). Sex is God's gift for love and procreation, but only in the confines of marriage (1 Corinthians 6:18). Do we live for God's pleasure, or are we more eager to satisfy our physical cravings?

....

'I, by your great mercy, will come into your house; in reverence will I bow down towards your holy temple' (Psalm 5:7).

ALeT

93

Fearing God or human knowledge

Where are the wise? Where are the scholars? Where are the philosophers of this age? Has not God made foolish the wisdom of the world?

The atheist–Christianity debate is not new. In recent years, however, the aggressive fundamentalist arguments against our faith have infiltrated susceptible minds which are easily impressed by scientific evidence purporting to negate the existence of God (despite the errors and superficiality found in certain of those texts). Even some novelists have used their skill and literary technique to undermine core principles and foundations of our faith; subtly drip-feeding humanist heresy into the unsuspecting reader. And I confess, it does make me cross!

In the past, however, it has also made me afraid—fearful that I might be wrong in my understanding, belief and experience of God, the risen Lord Jesus and the Holy Spirit. My school-level science will never stand up to the expertise of those who excel in this area. That said, I have learnt much and my faith has been encouraged by Christians whom God has called and equipped to work and witness in the scientific arena, many of whom have earned due respect for the eminent positions they've achieved in their particular fields.

Whether we are scientists or not, we are called to fear God and not human understanding. Our knowledge will always be imperfect and limited to our mortal appreciation of a divinely created and ordered world. So if your fear of God is being challenged by a fear of human intellect, make time to savour an extended faith-building word from our awesome Lord, by reading and reflecting on Job 36:22—37:13 and 38:1—41:34. May your faith, fear and wonder at his might and wisdom be richly edified, for 'he will be the sure foundation for your times, a rich store of salvation and wisdom and knowledge; the fear of the Lord is the key to this treasure' (Isaiah 33:6).

....

I praise you, God, that your ways and thoughts are so much higher than our own, your deeds too wonderful to comprehend. I stand in awe of your omniscient being.

ALeT

Fearing God to 'reap' his blessing

Fear the Lord your God… so that it may go well with you… 'The Lord commanded us to obey all these decrees and to fear the Lord our God, so that we might always prosper.'

When I was young, my motive for helping around the house was, at times, simply to earn some pocket money. In my teens, I spent hours getting dressed and made up, hoping to 'earn' a young man's attention. Newly married, I'd scour the house to 'earn' my in-laws' favour (quite unnecessarily, I might add!). Even now, under God's penetrating gaze, I'm convicted of certain traits that drive me to do things to 'earn' someone's approval.

The Israelites were urged to fear and obey God 'so that' it would go well with them. Nowadays, however, we don't tend to equate our Christian faith with 'earning' anything, 'for it is by grace you have been saved, through faith—and this not from yourselves, it is the gift of God—not by works, so that no one can boast' (Ephesians 2:8–9). Nevertheless, we do still reap what we sow (Galatians 6:8–9). If we sow tomato seeds, we will reap tomatoes. If we sow our lives with the fear of God, we will reap God's promised blessings.

We've already looked at a few examples of the fear of God in context and reflected on the consequent blessings. But for those days when we're struggling to trust his love and purpose and are tempted to do things our own way, let's recall the following list and look up the promises God has made to instruct, protect, provide, love, guide, help, bless, prosper, sustain, fulfil, satisfy, honour and forgive those who fear him: Psalm 25:12; 33:18–19; 34:7–9; 103:11–13; 111:5, 10; 115:11, 13; 128:1–2; 145:19; Proverbs 1:7; 19:23; 22:4; Luke 1:50.

If you have time, you may like to write out some of these verses to keep as a handy prompt—and so may your hearts and wills be encouraged by their truths.

....

Lord, thank you for your patience when my love for you falters, and for your longing to bless me through the life you intended me to live.

ALeT

Fearing the awesomeness of God

In the council of the holy ones God is greatly feared; he is more awesome than all who surround him. O Lord God Almighty, who is like you? You are mighty, O Lord, and your faithfulness surrounds you... Blessed are those who have learned to acclaim you.

'Who among the gods is like you, O Lord? Who is like you—majestic in holiness, awesome in glory, working wonders?' (Exodus 15:11). The word 'awesome' crops up regularly in my godson's vocabulary, especially when he's trying out his latest piece of gadgetry: 'Wow—awesome!' I too am prone to a whispered 'awesome' when faced with magnificent landscapes from the peaks and promontories of the Cotswold hills.

The intrinsic biblical meaning of 'awesome', however, has been lost somewhat in modern language, and we may find ourselves using it only in terms of describing God—his power, beauty and so on. In fact, the Hebrew word for 'awesome' implies a revelation of God that inspires fear. The 'awesomeness' of God is a quality that we need to respond to with the fear, reverence, awe and wonder he deserves.

Learning to fear God is an ongoing process. As we meditate on his awesomeness through prayer and his word, God himself will teach and inspire us to fear him (Deuteronomy 4:10; Jeremiah 32:39–40), to keep us from sinning and to enable us to reap his promised blessings. So let's determine to spend regular time acknowledging the awesome characteristics of God, responding both with wondrous worship spoken from our lips and with a life that upholds his ways.

A meaningful response to God in worship is the best way to put the world back into perspective. It focuses our hearts on God's awesome righteousness, authority, purpose and presence, which then counters our other 'fears'. In turn, we shall be inspired to fear him only, and so to experience fullness of life in ever increasing measure.

....

With my lips, I declare, 'How awesome is the Lord Most High, the great King over all the earth!' (Psalm 47:2), and with my life I determine to fear you.

Read Psalm 103:17 to see one of the greatest consequences of fearing God.

ALeT

Sandra Wheatley writes:

Is there more to looking than meets the eye? I wonder! The Bible is full of stories of people who were on the look-out, who were looking for the coming of their Redeemer, looking for a promise, looking for a lost son, a lost coin or a lost sheep. It all started in the garden of Eden, when God went looking for Adam and Eve in the cool of the day...

We can look at or look for something for ages. (If you've ever asked a man to look for something, you'll know what I mean!) But there is the subtlest of differences between looking and seeing. Sometimes I 'see' more when I close my eyes. The pictures in my imagination and memory can transport me beyond the daily grind. Something wonderful happens to my soul and spirit, and I soar like the eagle in Isaiah 40:31.

These days, there seem to be ever more constraints on my life. At times, my wheelchair feels like an implement of torture, as my one remaining talent, for sitting, has become an altogether excruciating affair due to painful areas in delicate parts. So I lie on my bed, gaze out of my window and look at the garden. It is simply a few conifer trees and a couple of unidentified bushes—I'm no horticulturist—but as I look out and begin to pray, my mind's eye takes me to various people and places, and I recognise again the essential part of me that cannot be constrained or contained.

A new perspective comes as God lifts me and carries me to places only he and I know about. These are no flights of fancy; nor are they visions and dreams like those experienced by people far more spiritual than I; but he lifts me and lets me catch a glimpse of the life beyond, of a day when we shall see him as he sees us.

Our vision is marred by many things. Mine certainly is. But I know what it is to close my eyes and really see!

What did God see?

God saw all that he had made, and it was very good.

When was the last time someone looked at you and said how lovely you are? When did someone look at you in such a way that you felt accepted, loved, cherished and of immense worth—so much so that it didn't matter that your make-up hadn't quite made it or the skin you're in doesn't quite fit any more?

Some days, I hardly recognise the person who looks back at me from the bathroom mirror. Despite my attempts at slopping and slapping on the creams, the lines remain and the downward descent of cheek to jowl continues. But these verses give me a glimpse of the worth and potential that God sees in each of us.

The creation story tells of God speaking everything into being—the heavens and earth and every plant and animal springing to life just because of his word. But for humankind God had something altogether different in mind.

Why would God go through this elaborate ritual? Why would he do something so complicated, when all he had to do was speak and the man would be formed? Only for us did God get down on his hands and knees to bring life. He took the dust of the earth and formed a man from it with his own hands, shaping and moulding, making an ear, an arm and a leg—all bearing his imprint as well as his image. Humankind became the pinnacle of creation. When he had finished, he looked… and he saw… and he knew that it was very good!

God breathed his life into humankind, and that incredible combination of dust and deity continues today in you and me. He hasn't stopped looking at you in the same way since!

....

You are someone special. You are a unique, once-only expression of the living God—made to hear, see and know him as no one else ever did, and then, out of that knowledge, to unveil to a watching world the revelation of God that only you can bring.

SW

What did Abram see?

Then the Lord took Abram outside and said to him, 'Look up into the sky and count the stars if you can. That's how many descendants you will have.'

From Genesis 12 to 25 the story of Abram unfolds. Thirteen chapters chart his life of faith and the coming of God's promise, and when we meet him here in chapter 15 he is meeting again with God and being comforted by those familiar words, 'Do not be afraid' (v. 1). This is the first time in the Bible that they are spoken by God (and it won't be the last).

Abram was at a low ebb. He had retreated to his tent and begun to languish in his fear that perhaps he would not see the fulfilment of God's promise to him after all (Genesis 13:14–17). Reality bites! But God didn't leave him there, even though Abram may have felt as if his pleas were just hitting the roof of his tent, just as we may feel that ours hit the ceiling at times. God appeared and asked Abram to step outside.

There are two vantage points in this story. Abram was focusing on his own inability and circumstances, so God gave him a different vantage point by taking him outside. Abram saw the heavens and heard the promise once again: his descendants would outnumber even the stars. Sometimes I need to be shown a different vantage point. My faith gets squashed to fit the size of the room I'm in. Then I need the help of God to take my eyes off my circumstances and to refocus them on his promise.

We do seem to inhabit a strange place sometimes, don't we— between our human circumstances and the promise of God? Abram was to wait another 14 years for the fulfilment of the promise God gave him. I've held a promise in my heart for years. I'm sure you have too—something longed for and yet to be fulfilled. Hang on!

....

Father God, when the days are tough, help us to yield to your invitation to be shown a different vantage point—your view, your promise and your presence.

SW

What did Moses see?

'This is the land I promised on oath to Abraham, Isaac and Jacob…
I have now allowed you to see it with your own eyes, but you will
not enter the land.'

As Moses climbed Pisgah peak on Mount Nebo, the most incredible
vista opened up before him—the promised land. After all the years of
bickering and battling, after all the years of wandering and warfare,
he finally saw it—but he wouldn't be allowed to step into it. In Num-
bers 20:1–13 we read why he couldn't take that final step.

I wonder what he was thinking as looked at the lands before him,
knowing that one incident had sealed his fate and he wouldn't be
the one who would lead God's people to the place of promise. Dare
we imagine that Moses saw the promised land and thought, 'If only
I hadn't struck that rock…'? For Moses, it seemed like a momentary
lapse of faith; for you and me, the equivalent may be, 'If only I hadn't
said… I hadn't done… I hadn't been there…'.

When I was younger, I used to entertain the notion that I would
live my life without any regrets. I would do all I could with all I had,
with God's help, taking any and every opportunity to serve him and
squeeze this life until the pips squeaked! I tried, but I failed. Moses
failed. Perhaps you've failed, too. But if ever there was a demonstra-
tion of just what grace is all about, and what Jesus did for you and me
on the cross, here it is.

The result of Moses' failure was that God did not allow him to step
into the promised land. God's judgment was final. My failure was
taken to the cross and to Jesus: I'm forgiven, and even the accusing
memories that sometimes pop up are hidden in his sea of forgetfulness as he says, 'What sin?' His grace is complete.

....

If you are carrying a burden of 'If only…', come to Jesus. His
forgiveness, mercy and grace are yours—your promised land of
wholeness and forgiveness.

SW

What did Elijah's servant see?

The servant went and looked, then returned to Elijah and said, 'I didn't see anything.'

I really do appreciate the honesty of Elijah's servant in this short passage. He and Elijah had climbed back to the summit of Mount Carmel. The first time, it just seemed to be a matter of obeying God and fire fell down instantly from heaven (18:20–39). Now we have the same Elijah, on the same mountain, being just as obedient, but things are not progressing in quite the same way.

As well as appreciating the honesty of the servant, I am challenged by the perseverance of Elijah in prayer. He prayed seven times, and seven times he sent his servant to go and look towards the sea. Elijah knew that the promised rain was coming—he says as much to Ahab in verse 41—but I wonder how he felt after three or four times of being told, 'I didn't see anything'. I wonder, too, how the servant felt, having to come back again and again to admit that there was nothing to see. Yet they both kept on doing what they were doing—praying and looking.

So often, that's all there is for us to do. The promise has been given—a promise of healing, of salvation for loved ones, of relief from hard or dry times. We live as people of the promise, don't we? But then something happens: we see or feel something out there on the horizon, and something inside us shifts as the tiny flame of hope ignites again.

The timing of such events always mystifies me, but I'm learning to be more honest about seeing the 'nothings' as I pray and look. I'm learning more and more that my honesty drives me closer to God and moulds me into being more like Jesus.

....

Lord, I'm learning that hope will always be there. It may be battered and misshapen, but you have promised to handle it, and me, with the utmost care. Thank you!

SW

What did the blind man see?

'You have seen him,' Jesus said, 'and he is speaking to you!'

John 9 is a fabulous chapter. It is given over entirely to the story of one blind man's healing and the impact that it had on his family, his community and the religious leaders of the day. The story contains some wonderfully comedic scenes, so it's well worth reading the whole chapter if you have time today. I hope you notice, too, that just as God got his hands dirty in making humankind, Jesus did the same when he healed this man (v. 6). Like Father, like Son!

After all the commotion that followed his healing, even being thrown out of the synagogue, Jesus seeks out the man. This would have been the first time he actually saw Jesus, as his healing had taken place away at the Pool of Siloam.

I have no idea what Jesus looked like. Even with the many depictions of him on film and TV, I still find it really hard to 'see' him. One thing I'm sure of, though: he didn't have a 'ready-brek' glow or a halo wafting above his head. As Isaiah foretells, 'There was nothing beautiful or majestic about his appearance, nothing to attract us to him' (Isaiah 53:2): Jesus seems to have been a very ordinary-looking man—so much so that he had to identify himself as the Son of Man (v. 37).

I've lost count of the times in my life when I have encountered Jesus. It still happens: he still shows up in unexpected places, in unexpected lives. He still seeks me out when I have need of him, and reveals himself in the lives of those who care so much for me that they take the time to visit, to phone, to email, to be with me. As we share and pray together, or chatter and giggle, I'm always reminded of these words: 'You have seen him… and he is speaking to you.'

....

Look out for Jesus today. He'll seek you out; he'll come and find you. You'll see him in unexpected places and faces, and when you do… just smile!

SW

What did Jesus see?

As he approached Jerusalem and saw the city, he wept over it.

I love seeing a city skyline, especially at night. I've had the opportunity to see many across the world, but my favourite view remains Durham city, by day or night. There's a particular view from a particular approach road that I never tire of showing visitors and friends. My heart swells with pride as they gaze in wonder at the majestic sight of the cathedral and castle.

As Jesus approached Jerusalem on Palm Sunday, the cheers and celebrations of the crowd will have been ringing in his ears. Their king had come, but, for Jesus, the emotion of it all perhaps became too much. He not only saw the city ahead of him, but he also knew that his days were numbered. He saw the city he loved, and cried as he understood not only his own fate but the city's future too (vv. 43–44).

What Jesus saw in the city he loved, we too can see in the cities around the world that, despite the bright lights and attractions, have an underbelly of deprivation and distress, of sin and the need for redemption. Thank God for the ministry of the Street Pastors who are making such a difference in each and every city where they are based. Thank God for the tears we cry, as well as the prayers we pray for our cities to be transformed. I truly believe that we, as Christians, can bring about that transformation by our practical care and work.

We need to be moved as Jesus was. We need to move as Jesus did—towards the challenge of the city. For Jesus, it meant his death. Who knows what it may mean for us—but I'm convinced that our cities will be changed as we continue to take the light of the gospel into their dark places.

....

Father God, enable us to see beyond the bright lights that can blind us to the darkness and need in city life. Help us to pray more effectively for them to know your love.

SW

What did the Roman centurion see?

When the Roman officer who stood facing him saw how he had died, he exclaimed, 'This man truly was the Son of God!'

In all probability, this wasn't the first and wouldn't be the last crucifixion that the Roman centurion attended, but this one was different. What he saw caused him to proclaim that Jesus was the Son of God.

All he had seen was the way in which Jesus died. He may never have seen any of Jesus' miracles or heard his sermons, or seen the impact that Jesus had on those who followed him. He only witnessed his death. So what did he see and why did it evoke such a response?

This Roman officer will have taken part in the humiliation and shame of Jesus, making sure he was stripped naked before being nailed to the cross. He will have heard the crowd scoffing and taunting Jesus. He will have seen Jesus' mother and his disciple John looking on in horror. He will have seen the abject suffering of a man who, for no 'crime' other than being 'the King of the Jews', was dying before his eyes. He will have seen Jesus at the lowest point in his life, in the moments before he died—responding to the taunts with compassion and forgiveness, reaching out, even while pinned to a cross, to offer forgiveness.

There are times when our lives are being watched by others. The way we react in and through the hard times can have a profound effect on those people. I'm constantly amazed that it is in the difficult days that the most opportunities come to share Jesus with others. It's when I'm at my lowest and weakest, and feel the worst, that God is often most clearly seen.

Sometimes, the truth of our belief is best seen in pain, and faith is at its best through the worst of times.

Lord God, through the best of times or worst of times, please shine through my life. I long to be more like Jesus.

SW

What would it be like to see your life and the people you meet daily in the way that God sees them? When there are no seats left on the train or bus after a busy day, and noisy children are irritating... love is patient. When a spiteful person leaves you in the lurch, then comes to ask for your help... love is kind. Love is not irritable or resentful. As Paul tells the Corinthians, love does not rejoice in wrongdoing but rejoices in the truth.

When a close friend is invited to a party and has a wonderful time without you, or gains the promotion you wanted... love is not envious.

When you are successful... love is not boastful or arrogant. Love is not rude. It does not insist on its own way. These are tough principles to put into practice at times.

Love sees beyond the obvious. A story is told of a situation on a train where a dad seemed to be letting his children run riot. A fellow passenger became irritated, wanting the children to be kept under control; another knew the story behind their behaviour. They were on their way home from the hospital where their mum had just died.

When God looks at our world, he sees the bigger picture. He sees the hurts behind the spiteful behaviour of a colleague or the angry reaction of a friend.

Last week Sandra Wheatley helped us to see as Jesus sees. Over the next week, Liz Pacey challenges us to live as God wants. As you go through the coming week, ask God to give you his eyes to see the world around you, and then follow Jesus' example, living a life that pleases God.

Living as God wants

'The Lord disciplines those he loves, and he punishes everyone he accepts as a child.' Endure hardship as discipline; God is treating you as children. For what children are not disciplined by their parents?

What comes to mind when we hear the word 'discipline'? It's not an easy word. Perhaps we remember an angry parent or teacher, punishing us for doing something wrong or setting rules where we just didn't see the point.

Although it was more than 30 years ago, I'll never forget the stern face sitting across the table from me when I went for my interview to become a student nurse at a prestigious Edinburgh hospital: 'You won't just be able to go and meet your mother on Princes Street at any time you like, you know.' I was accepted for training and, after the four previous glorious years of being an undergraduate and doing pretty much as I liked (I did get a degree at the end of it!), discipline had arrived in my life.

Since then, of course, I've realised that discipline comes in many shapes and forms, sometimes painful, sometimes very necessary. In our Christian lives we learn its importance—and we'll look at that a bit more closely over the next few days—but we also see that God disciplines us for a reason. He does it out of love, and because he wants the very best for us. He wants us to share in his holiness (v. 10).

Today's passage talks about running the race marked out for us (v. 1). I'd always planned to be a teacher, but that day in Edinburgh I set off in faith on the race God had marked out for me. Sometimes it was hard, and I needed perseverance to carry on. Sometimes I grew weary, and it was hard not to lose heart (v. 3), but behind it all was the knowledge of God's love for me, and that kept me right on track.

....

Thank you, Lord, for your hand on my life, guiding me and loving me—especially in the times when I can't quite see the way ahead.

LP

Precious time

'Seek first his kingdom and his righteousness, and all these things will be given to you as well. Therefore do not worry about tomorrow, for tomorrow will worry about itself. Each day has enough trouble of its own.'

I love reading novels, and I've always rather fancied myself as a romantic heroine who has nothing to do all day but embroider and read (well, perhaps miss out the embroidery…). It's the leisurely lifestyle I crave, and yes, I know I've got my rose-tinted glasses on here. Few of us today have that luxury.

Sometimes, though, I have an uncomfortable suspicion that I could have a much more relaxed life if I were more disciplined in the way I use my time. However, before I am able to achieve that lifestyle, I need to realise what a precious gift God is giving me. Do we always see God as being in charge of our time? Do we ask him about new activities before we take them on? If we don't, we can waste a lot of time in worrying about all sorts of things. In our passage today, Jesus is showing us that we really need to put him and his kingdom first, and then other things will follow on naturally.

I ended up in hospital for a few days recently. It was a real wake-up call for me. Other people had to take over the stuff I'd planned to do—and, guess what, they did it. I had to admit that I wasn't indispensable! At times in our lives, we need to be gentle with ourselves and not give ourselves too punishing a timetable. We need to learn to say 'No' and schedule in time for ourselves. We have to plan ahead in some areas of life—it would be irresponsible not to—but there is a lot to be said for living in the moment, as Jesus advises.

When we truly give our lives over to God we will value our time a lot more and get more out of it.

Read Psalm 31:14–20 and praise God for his unfailing love.

LP

Time for God?

For this reason, since the day we heard about you, we have not stopped praying for you and asking God to fill you with the knowledge of his will through all spiritual wisdom and understanding.

As Christians, we spend a lot of time praying and reading the Bible. Or do we? Much as we love God, sometimes we just don't seem to get around to it. Of course, some of us have more time than others. Perhaps illness or lack of employment leaves us with too many empty hours. Sometimes it's even harder to get motivated to take time for God when a whole long day stretches before us than when we're frantically busy.

Whatever our situation, we need to practise the discipline of making time for God—but it mustn't be just because we feel guilty. Our desire to be in his presence should be a natural consequence of our love for him. We may be able to spend only a few minutes consciously in his presence, but God still sees our hearts. The more time we spend with him, the more we'll crave, and the more creative we'll be in making that space to be with him.

We may cry out that we really don't have enough time, but we need to distinguish between genuine reasons and excuses. Are we sometimes frightened to meet with God, worried about what we might hear if we really open ourselves up to him? If that is the case, then we're not seeing him as a loving heavenly Father, and we need to be honest with him about that. The only way we will find spiritual wisdom and understanding (v. 9) is by taking time to get to know God better.

There are a lot of different ways of being with God in prayer, and today's passage is a beautiful example of how we can bring the people we love into his presence.

....

Read the passage again, and rejoice in and pray for those people who are special to you.

LP

Time for friends

Dear friends, since God so loved us, we also ought to love one another. No one has ever seen God; but if we love one another, God lives in us and his love is made complete in us.

What a privilege it is to have people to love! I was 36 when I met my husband and in the preceding years I was so thankful (and, of course, still am!) for the blessing of close friends. Our lives can be very lonely without them.

As we move through different stages of life, our friendships don't remain static. I've known some of my friends since childhood; others have come on the scene much later. There are all sorts of degrees of friendship, but one thing I have learnt over the years is that the best ones have to be worked at, and they involve a certain amount of discipline if they are to flourish. We can't take our friends for granted: neglecting them may mean losing them. We have to be prepared to make sacrifices sometimes, learning to put our friends first and being there for them, whatever the cost is to ourselves. Friendship is a precious flower that needs nurturing; it doesn't just arrive fully grown.

It's wonderful having Christian friends because our faith brings a very special and deep dimension to the relationship, but we mustn't exclude people who don't share our beliefs. Some years ago, I heard a saying that has stayed with me ever since: 'Make a friend, be a friend, bring a friend to Jesus'. God can put all kinds of unlikely people in our path and, although we wouldn't or shouldn't set out to befriend someone just to 'convert' them, it is really special if that person does finally come to understand how our lives are blessed by knowing the love of Jesus, and experiences it for themselves.

....

Lord, please help me to be sensitive to the needs of my friends and be ready to put real effort into growing my friendships.

LP

Honouring God

Honour the lord with your wealth, with the firstfruits of all your crops; then your barns will be filled to overflowing, and your vats will brim over with new wine.

As a student nurse, time management wasn't the only discipline I learnt. There was financial management, too. Because we were over the magic age of 21, four of us were allowed to move quickly out of the nurses' home and find a flat. As we were earning a real wage for the first time ever, it was a bit of a bore having to put so much aside for rent and food, but it had to be done.

In today's economic climate, money worries are often to the fore. As Christians, we have a responsibility to use our money wisely, however much or little we may have. If we're on a tight budget, we have no choice but to be disciplined about how much we spend, unless we want to end up in debt. I must admit, these days, I sometimes struggle with the realisation of how much money I used to fritter away when I had a bigger disposable income. Part of our discipline, as far as money goes, must be to remain realistic about what we actually need as opposed to what we think we need, or want. Perhaps, too, that discipline involves being more grateful for what we already have and creative in the way we use and care for it.

Our passage today gives us a foolproof way of managing our money. We are to give to God the best we have to offer, not the leftovers. Then we will never be short of anything we need—quite the reverse, in fact.

In keeping God's commandments, we will find true wealth (v. 2), and will realise that there are more important things than money—love and faithfulness, for example (v. 3).

....

Is there any way I'm failing to honour God with my money or possessions?

Read Luke 6:37–42 to learn more about how God wants us to live.

LP

Looking after our bodies

I know that there is nothing better for people than to be happy and do good while they live. That each of them may eat and drink, and find satisfaction in all their toil—this is the gift of God.

'How long did you manage on the treadmill?' asked the doctor as he stood at the foot of my hospital bed. 'Oh, about half an hour,' I answered airily, knowing full well it hadn't been anywhere near that. He consulted his notes: 'Three minutes,' he smiled. I was mortified. I honestly hadn't realised I'd been quite that pathetic.

Thoughts of a lifelong diet of lettuce leaves flashed through my mind, along with an image of myself in a pink Lycra tracksuit, pounding away at a gym. Then sense returned. I did need to change my lifestyle for the good of my health. I did need some sort of discipline in my eating and exercise, but I knew that balance was going to be the answer. Our reading today tells us that eating, drinking and finding satisfaction in work are God's gifts. We need to strive towards that balanced lifestyle.

A good friend of mine outlined her action plan to me recently. She called it the 3x3: three meals and three portions of fruit and vegetables a day, and three good walks a week. That struck me as being very sensible. She wasn't committing to anything that she couldn't realistically achieve, but she would be disciplining herself enough to make a steady and noticeable change to her health, starting small and building up. That is an important focus for us in many of the disciplines of life. Remember the fable about the tortoise and the hare? Slow and steady wins the day.

Sometimes we like to make a show of the changes we are making, but if we just get on with what God asks of us, quietly and consistently, we will win through in the end.

....

Lord, please help me to trust you with the small things of my life as well as the big.

LP

A new mindset

You were taught, with regard to your former way of life, to put off your old self, which is being corrupted by its deceitful desires; to be made new in the attitude of your minds; and to put on the new self, created to be like God.

Perhaps we're struggling with negative thoughts about discipline—worrying that it involves giving things up, and seeing God as someone who cracks the whip and takes all the fun out of life. At first, today's Bible passage may make us feel even more like that. It seems to be a whole catalogue of 'Do not's (vv. 25–31). They all have our best interests at heart, but seeing them listed like that makes discipline look very daunting. Before this list, however, is a wonderful 'Do...' which makes all the rest possible. We are to put on a new self, created to be like God (v. 24). How amazing is that?

Sometimes we look at ourselves and shy away from what we see. Perhaps we feel powerless to change. We might just need to see ourselves as God sees us and learn to love ourselves as we are. Or, if we see that change really is necessary, God can give us the power to make it happen.

I recently went on a 'Learning to listen' course. At the end of each session, we split into pairs and took turns at listening to each other. After I'd finished talking to my listener about some changes I felt I needed to make in my life, she asked me how I was feeling about what I'd said. I had to admit that I wasn't sure I was actually ready to make these necessary changes. Then it dawned on me that I needed to stop talking about it and get on and ask God to give me the power to do it.

Changing things in our lives can involve a lot of spiritual and practical effort, but it's worth it—and we're worth it!

Lord, help me to come before you honestly, to see myself as you see me and be prepared for you to make me new where necessary.

LP

Fiona Barnard writes:

I am currently in Asia, far from home. After three months of living out of a suitcase, being bombarded by foreign sights and sounds takes its toll. I am longing for home—where I am known and loved and secure, where things make sense, where I belong. For now, though, I am living in exile.

Janice became a Christian last week. At last, the gospel makes sense of her life. She belongs to Jesus and to his kingdom. She is floating on air—but then she lands with a bump. Her boyfriend does not share her enthusiasm for Jesus. Her colleagues inform her that religion is 'unscientific'. Her mother reminds her that prayer never gets the dishes washed or the clothes ironed. Janice has to understand that the world is not at home with a life of faith in Jesus. As a Christian, Janice is living in exile.

Nancy is in despair. She has prayed and prayed for her husband to become a Christian, for her teenage daughter to calm down and for her neighbours to be less aggressive, but heaven is silent. She is depressed and wonders if God cares. Nancy is living in exile.

May recognises that she has allowed ambition to override all other priorities in her life. She has compromised her faith in the decisions she has made to climb the career ladder. Sometimes she misses Christian fellowship and the closeness she once felt to Jesus, but not enough to change her ways. May is living in exile.

In the sixth century BC, God's people were in exile, far from home. They had thought that their special relationship with God made them safe and secure, but now they had no home, no land, no identity, no place of worship and no hope. We too are in exile, far from the centre of God's kingdom of light and truth. For each of us, there are different reasons for feeling far from God—personal circumstances; factors that are beyond our control, such as illness or certain types of medication; our sin or that of others. All of us, while we live on this earth, are far from our heart's home, which is the full presence of Jesus. And so, God's word to his devastated people can speak to us too. Over the next couple of weeks, we will listen to the prophets Ezekiel and Jeremiah, and we will see how believers like Daniel lived faithfully, far from home.

I pray that God meet with you, even in exile. 'O Lord, in all generations you have been our home' (Psalm 90:1, CEV).

In exile, pray your feelings

By the rivers of Babylon we sat and wept when we remembered Zion… How can we sing the songs of the Lord while in a foreign land? If I forget you, Jerusalem, may my right hand forget its skill… Remember, Lord, what the Edomites did on the day Jerusalem fell.

God had uprooted me and taken me to a place I didn't want to be. I was heartbroken and furious. I sulked and refused to talk to him. But in the months and years that followed, when I felt as if God had disappeared from my life, I discovered a longing for him in the deepest part of my being. Those exile years shook me to the core. My faith was dismantled and eventually built up again, piece by piece.

When we are in exile, for whatever reason, it is not only natural to express our feelings, it is imperative. If we needed any confirmation of that, this psalm is a good start. The song describes God's people weeping in their desolation. The river beside which they sit seems to have collected a great mass of tears, flowing endlessly. They have hung their harps on trees because they can no longer praise God (v. 2). The centre of worship in Jerusalem is destroyed and, anyway, they don't have the heart: God is too far away. And yet, as they lament their loss, they also discover their deep longing for God's city, for God's presence. They vow loyalty.

Amid the tears, there is also fierce anger: their enemies have made them suffer. The shocking image of dashing infants against rocks (v. 9) speaks of their desire for vengeance. This is not a song we often sing in church.

Pain and hatred are powerful emotions, and where better to take them than to God? These feelings are too raw to be 'polite', yet their inclusion in the Bible indicates that God takes them seriously and accepts them as an authentic reaction to suffering. Nothing is too awful to be beyond his care.

....

If you are in exile today, tell God how you feel. He knows anyway: he's heard it before. Don't pretend to him or yourself. 'Much better to say it to his face than behind his back,' we say, so be real. He understands.

FB

In exile, watch and warn

Ezekiel, son of man, I have appointed you to stand watch for the people of Israel. So listen to what I have to say, and then warn them for me... You must warn them to turn from their sinful ways so they won't be punished.

'Broken Britain': that is what the politicians have called a country that was once named 'great'. They point to poverty and family dysfunction, to gun crime and antisocial behaviour. Researchers and sociologists and spin doctors are paid large amounts of money to come up with schemes and solutions and policies to 'fix broken Britain'. What would you suggest if they asked you?

The people of Israel were broken. The Babylonians had reduced their capital city to rubble and taken most people into exile. Ezekiel the priest was among them. With the destruction of the temple, he could not do his job of offering sacrifices. And yet, amid the ruins of his personal and professional life, God gave him a new task: Ezekiel was called to be a prophet, to speak God's word to a broken people.

Many 'prophets' around that time were trying to encourage Israel, saying that because they were God's special people, they would soon be home. However, God's message through Ezekiel was not so optimistic. In essence, they were 'stubborn and hard-headed' (2:4) and they were reaping the results of their behaviour. The exile was their punishment. They had to change their ways.

A watchman is usually a strong man whose job is to stay awake and look out for danger. You may feel weak. You may think, like Ezekiel, that you are not qualified. And yet, if you have experienced God's life in you, you have something valuable to share—an insight into what is happening around you. You understand how actions can have destructive consequences. Might God be calling you, as a Christian in this broken society, to keep watch and speak his words?

....

Lord, help me to watch and warn so that I can be an agent of healing amid the brokenness of this society.

Read Matthew 5:13–16 to see Jesus' imaginative way of giving a similar message.

FB

In exile, seek God's presence

'Those who worship idols will be punished and get what they deserve…' After the Lord had finished speaking, the winged creatures spread their wings… The brightness of the Lord's glory above them left Jerusalem and stopped at a hill east of the city.

I used to look out for an old derelict church on my bus journey. An enormous red-brick building, its once beautiful windows were all boarded up. Slates were adrift from the roof. A massive padlock kept its rusty gate closed, and nailed to the flaking front door was a notice, 'Danger! Work in progress!' Every time, I was struck by the irony of it: the church was a scene of utter devastation. Nothing at all was in progress apart from rot.

What had happened to that church? Its grandeur indicated a once-vibrant congregation. In its heyday, old and young would have piled in through those gates. The rafters would have vibrated with worship. The stained-glass windows would have lit up the stories of Jesus, inviting those outside to come in. What went wrong with this and so many other churches?

In a vision, God took Ezekiel back to Jerusalem (chs. 8—11). What he was shown was not the physical but the spiritual desecration of the temple. In the space built for the worship of the one almighty Creator, he saw people worshipping the sun and animal gods. On the site where the invisible God, who is everywhere, chose to meet his special people, pagan idols had been erected. Israel had broken her covenant with God, choosing to serve other gods, and so God's glory, the sign of his presence, departed, driven out by rebellion.

In the West, where church decline is a sad reality, this is worth pondering. Where God's presence has not been acknowledged, his glory has left. Where people have been distracted from their priorities, minor issues have dominated and strangled life.

....

The encouragement, both then and now, is that God's glory travels east to Babylon. God is not confined to the temple: he goes to those in exile. But he hovers for a moment on a hill, the Mount of Olives, where, 500 years later, Jesus was to promise, 'I am with you always!'

FB

In exile, listen for truth

They lie to good people and encourage them to do wrong, and they convince the wicked to keep sinning and ruin their lives... If they sin by worshipping idols and then go to a prophet to find out what I say, I will give them the answer their sins deserve. When they hear my message, perhaps they will see that they need to turn back to me.

How would the somewhat eccentric Ezekiel go down in your church today? He messes with his beard. He digs a tunnel out of his house rather than using the door. He lies on his side for a year and eats food cooked in cow dung. He refuses to grieve over his wife's death, and can see things happening 500 miles away. He could easily be dismissed as a lunatic.

Ezekiel is strange, and his message is bleak, blaming the people for the mess they are in. Things are bad enough, you might argue, without this madman preaching damnation. Yet the Bible holds him up as a true prophet, speaking God's word, swimming against the tide. In Ezekiel 12—14, false prophets are condemned.

When things are rough and people are suffering, it is natural to try to make things better. Yet this attempt is empty if it simply masks the real problem and encourages people to avoid facing the consequences of their decisions. If there is a cancer growing in me, it is not kind just to cover it up or distract me. The best action may place me under the surgeon's knife, even though it will hurt.

God's message through Ezekiel reminds us not only that God uses all types of people, but also that his ultimate aim is for us to be restored to him. Until the idols, the pride and deceit, are seen for what they are, we cannot experience the true comfort that comes from a renewed relationship with God. When we are in exile, truth is kinder than flattery and empty words, however painful.

....

Lord, give me ears to hear your truth 'above the storms of passion, the murmurs of self will'.

Read 1 John 1:5–9 to witness a glorious mix of truth, forgiveness and restoration.

FB

In exile, remember the Lover

I covered your naked body with my own robe. Then I solemnly promised that you would belong to me and that I, the Lord God, would take care of you… You were as beautiful as a queen… You offered yourself to every passerby… an unfaithful wife who would rather have sex with strangers than with your own husband.

The first time I read Ezekiel 16, I was 20 and longing for love. The poetry at the beginning of this chapter filled me with wonder and warmth, as God describes his tender love for his exiled people.

It was so beautiful to read how God reached out to Jerusalem, a forgotten, unlovely scrap of humanity. His care, as he washed the blood from her and covered her with oil, carried a poignancy that moved me deeply. The generosity lavished upon her—clothes and sandals, bracelets and earrings, ring and crown—had an extravagance about it that spoke of God being besotted with his people. This was so different from the image of God as staid and sensible.

Then I encountered the devastation of betrayal. I read the doleful description of his beautiful bride chasing after anyone who would have her. I could feel the anger in God's voice as he spoke of her worshipping the gifts he had given to her and cheapening herself shamelessly. This was the nub of it: God's people had abandoned him. The exile was of their own making. They had broken their marriage covenant. God was not being vindictive. This ardent, emotional tale expressed his broken heart, a jealousy born of committed love, and a stunned incomprehension at such senseless choices.

It is easy to lose our first passion for Jesus, to be distracted by what he has given us and to look to others rather than him for the satisfaction of our deepest needs. And so we are exiled from the one who really loves us—truly, madly, deeply. When we are suffering, whether through our own fault or not, we need to remember our divine lover.

....

Lord, your love for me is overwhelming. Forgive my cold heart.

Read 1 John 3:1 for another expression of God's love for you.

FB

In exile, be content

Seek the peace and prosperity of the city to which I have carried you into exile. Pray to the Lord for it, because if it prospers, you too will prosper… When seventy years are completed for Babylon, I will… bring you back. For I know the plans I have for you… to give you hope and a future.

Sometimes there is no escape. You may be in a place where you are unknown and lonely. Your work may be dull or stressful, and all your job applications get nowhere. Perhaps you are in a painful relationship that wears you down. You long to be in a different place and wonder if you can survive any longer. Then you will understand a little of how the Jewish exiles felt, stuck in Babylonia against their will. They were away from everything familiar and comfortable. They wondered when the nightmare would end.

So it was a great comfort when prophets told them they would be home soon. They clung on to that hope and waited, a little in limbo. Then a letter arrived from Jeremiah. He had repeatedly warned them that their disobedience against God would result in punishment. Now he had a different message: he counselled them to settle down in Babylon, to plant vineyards, get married and have children. They should make the place of exile their home. They would be there for 70 years, a lifetime for many. That must have been hard to swallow.

But there was more: God said, 'I know the plans I have for you, plans to prosper you and not to harm you.' He had other purposes that his people could not see. There was a promise of hope and prosperity and a renewed relationship with him. These verses are a reminder that God has not forgotten us. While his timing is often different from our own, he calls us to trust him—not because he will take us out of our difficult places but because, somehow, amid our struggles, he is doing something in us. He can work for our good.

....

Dear Lord, help me to trust you even when I am not delivered from the things that afflict me. Teach me and use me, even in the places not of my choosing.

FB

In exile, select your compromises

'They must be healthy, handsome, clever, wise, educated, and fit to serve in the royal palace. Teach them how to speak and write our language and give them the same food and wine that I am served. Train them for three years, and then they can become court officials.'

'Should I watch this film… spend my money on that… enter into this relationship?' A few years ago, the idea that Christians should be 'in the world, but not of it' created a response with quite specific rules about what was considered godly (no pubs, no cinema, no dancing and so on). A re-evaluation of what is distinctive about Christ-centred behaviour has been necessary, but very challenging.

I wonder how Daniel and his friends felt as they were hauled from their own country and chosen to be students in their conquerors' regime. They were expected to assimilate the culture and forget their Jewish identity. Were they excited and energised or frightened and resentful? We are not told. These lads, the *crème de la crème* in their society, did not seem to object to the project. They underwent their studies, even though there were aspects, including astrology, that would not have accorded with their faith. They even accepted Babylonian names that honoured pagan gods—a very personal imposition.

However, for some reason, sharing in the king's food and wine was one step too far. The food may have been used in pagan sacrifices, but, whatever the issue, Daniel and his friends were not prepared to compromise. Their decision could have cost them their lives.

Living in a society that does not acknowledge our God, we are constantly being tested. Interestingly, it was a seemingly innocuous issue—gourmet food—that Daniel considered to be a challenge to his faith. It is often not the obvious temptations that lead us away from our primary commitment to Jesus, but the seemingly 'harmless' distractions that can cause us to 'abandon our first love'.

....

Dear Lord, show me the battles
I must fight and give me courage
not to compromise.

Read 1 Corinthians 10:31–33 to help you in your decision making.

FB

In exile, look from God's perspective

Daniel said, 'Pray that the God who rules from heaven will be merciful and explain this mystery, so that we and the others won't be put to death.' In a vision one night, Daniel was shown the dream and its meaning.

Perspective is everything. It determines whether you see lots of dots or a masterpiece. It leaves you terrified as a drill descends towards your face or glad that the rot is being taken from your tooth. It makes saying 'no' to a doughnut complete madness or wisdom personified. When we are in exile, our perspective will make all the difference to our experience.

Daniel was living in a land where the king's mood could be a matter of life or death for anyone in his path. An all-powerful pagan despot was frightening enough, but his fits of irrational rage added to the danger. A troubling dream had unleashed massive insecurity, and the king demanded not only an interpretation but also an account of the dream itself. Judging his advisers to be uncooperative, he decreed that all the wise men, including Daniel, must be put to death.

From Nebuchadnezzar's perspective, the great kingdom that he had built appeared to be under severe threat. It represented his whole identity, his dreams, his lifetime's achievement. It was all he had and all he was. Without it, he was desperate, irrational and terrified.

Daniel's perspective was different. He had never allowed the splendour of Babylon to cloud his outlook, even though it had reduced his own country to rubble. Despite his personal history, he held on to Israel's God as the King of kings, the all-knowing. And so, when Daniel was under a death sentence, he was resourceful and took control. While the king was reduced to panic, Daniel was confident in the sovereignty and guidance of Yahweh. He knew that God was merciful, and that made all the difference in the world.

....

Lord, in the minor and major disasters of this day, lift my eyes to see things from your perspective.

FB

In exile, learn his-story

'During the time of those kings, the God who rules from heaven will set up an eternal kingdom that will never fall. It will be like the stone that was cut from the mountain, but not by human hands—the stone that crushed the iron, bronze, clay, silver and gold.'

History teaches that nothing lasts. We are impressed by beautiful buildings and art, and awed by accounts of great civilisations. Yet the fact that they are in museums and libraries shows that those who were giants in their time are dead and gone. New wonders and new empires succeeded them and were themselves supplanted. The powerful are tempted to behave as though their success will never end, but ostentation, celebrity and incessant media hype can drown out uncomfortable uncertainties. In exile, it is worth remembering that the giants that overwhelm us today may be gone tomorrow.

During this exile, God did not confine his word to his own people. He spoke to pagan kings too, albeit with Daniel's interpretation. This may have surprised the Jewish community, but it came as a timely reminder that Yahweh was king of all the world.

Nebuchadnezzar, like many, believed that a statue expressed a ruler's greatness. To see an image shattered, beginning with its feet of clay, was shocking. Away from a court of flattery, he was facing his own mortality and the finality of his empire—crushed by the force of a stone 'not cut by human hands'. Almighty God was giving this pagan ruler the opportunity to invest his life in things of eternal significance that would outlast him. He was inviting him to bow the knee not to Daniel but to the King of kings, whose kingdom will never end.

Centuries later, who has left the greatest legacy: the exiled Daniel or the mighty Nebuchadnezzar? In exile, we need eyes of faith to see beyond the immediate powers to the everlasting kingdom that God is building among us.

Lord, as a Christian I often feel in the minority. Remind me today that with you I am in the majority.

Read 1 Peter 2:4–7 to see how this 'living stone' is carried into the New Testament.

FB

In exile, trust in God's sovereignty

'Praise and honour the King who rules from heaven! Everything he does is honest and fair, and he can shatter the power of those who are proud.'

'Our God reigns!' Christians assert, but when secret police raid homes to search for Bibles, it may be hard to believe. When death threats are made to believers who have chosen to be baptised, it may be tempting to question. When a church cannot get planning permission because the local authorities don't like Christians, we may wonder about the extent of God's power. Encouragingly, the faith of believers under severe persecution is often strengthened by God's grace, but there must be moments of doubt, when the immediate and seen appear more real than the ultimate and invisible.

Living in the magnificent city of Babylon, amid the grandeur and might of a pagan empire, the Jewish exiles could have concluded that human force and local gods ruled. The splendour of Yahweh, the Almighty God, who could not be represented by an idol, may have seemed like a distant, improbable memory. This testimony from Nebuchadnezzar would have been a huge boost to their faith, an encouragement to persevere. Here the all-powerful, successful king confesses how he had ignored the warning against pride that Yahweh had given him in a dream. It took beast-like madness to enable sanity to dawn. Brought to his knees, he acknowledged God as the Most High. His praise emerged from deep personal brokenness.

I remember a person being described as 'a self-made man who worshipped his creator'. Increasingly in our society, modesty is interpreted as a sign of weakness, while confidence and assertiveness indicate potential and ambition. May God grant us a humility that accepts who we are before 'the King who rules from heaven' and clings on to that faith despite all appearances.

....

'Your kingdom come. Your will be done on earth as it is in heaven.'
Repeat this prayer in faith as you go about your life today.

FB

In exile, stay outward-looking

'King Belshazzar, you knew all of this, but you still refused to honour the Lord who rules from heaven... You praised idols made of silver, gold, bronze, iron, wood and stone, even though they cannot see or hear or think. You refused to worship the God who gives you breath.'

'I want to come to your Bible study,' Ying said, 'so I can understand about British culture.' She is not alone in thinking that the God of the Bible is British and that the UK is a Christian country. I love explaining that most of the Bible was set in the Middle East and that God is the God of the whole world.

One of the lessons the Jewish people had failed to grasp was that Yahweh was the God of the whole earth and that their task was to draw even the Gentiles to him. Yet here in exile, far from the security of being in the majority, we see signs that their understanding is growing. Take this story. Although most of the Old Testament was written in Hebrew, this passage was in Aramaic, the language of the Persians, who defeated the Babylonian empire. It has been suggested that the story was originally produced as an evangelistic tract to tell the Gentiles about God. God's people were looking outward.

Belshazzar insulted God by using the sacred vessels from the temple for a drunken banquet. The king had heard about Nebuchadnezzar's acknowledgment of the Most High God after his period of madness, but he responded with contempt. Although Nebuchadnezzar had come to his senses, Belshazzar did not pay heed. The party ended in disarray and terror as God declared, through the ever-faithful and ageing Daniel, the consequences of the king's sacrilege. The might of the Babylonian empire came tumbling down.

God still calls faithful servants, young and old, to declare his sovereignty and holiness, his mercy and his judgment to the nations of the world. In exile, we mustn't forget the task of crosscultural mission.

....

Dear Lord, it is so easy to get caught up in my own world. Help me to live and speak so that nations of the earth will be drawn to you.

FB

In exile, keep talking to God

Daniel heard about the law, but when he returned home, he went upstairs and prayed in front of the window that faced Jerusalem. In the same way that he had always done, he knelt down in prayer three times a day, giving thanks to God.

'What is the point? I feel as if God has forgotten me.' When God seems far away, it is hard to pray. When our spiritual certainties have taken a knock, daily devotions can feel very dry and pointless. When we are surrounded by people who are indifferent or antagonistic to our faith, we can be tempted to compromise or even give up.

It would have been very easy for Daniel to abandon his Jewish faith, built, as it was, around the Jerusalem temple, with its priests and liturgy and special days. The physical ruins of the temple and city stood as a metaphor for the religion. Indeed, many had cried, 'How can we sing about the Lord in a foreign land?' because Judaism was so clearly focused on a particular place. Bearing God's punishment, they felt far from home and far from God.

Yet Daniel had put a routine in place to remind him that he was God's servant. He 'knelt down in prayer three times a day', although this custom was not prescribed by Judaism. Despite a demanding job as governor in Babylon, he made a point of withdrawing and acknowledging his allegiance to a greater authority than the Babylonian king, law and idols. Even the threat of lions did not deter him. The daily discipline, the kneeling, the choice of the window facing Jerusalem, all showed his determination to be faithful to Almighty God, who heard his prayers, even in that pagan environment.

When our feelings and circumstances militate against our sense of spiritual well-being, that is the time to cling to the facts of our faith. That is when routine and the discipline of daily devotion may hold us, even if our emotions do not. Even amid lions, God is with us.

....

At this stage, Daniel was an old man. What was the secret of his lifelong ministry and courageous faith amid the demands and success of his professional career?

FB

In exile, pray for renewal

Dry bones, listen to what the Lord is saying to you. 'I, the Lord God, will put breath in you, and once again you will live. I will wrap you with muscles and skin and breathe life into you. Then you will know that I am the Lord.'

'I am drained; I feel dead inside. I have nothing more to give.' She stared at her coffee cup, her eyes dull and resigned. 'All my enthusiasm for life and for serving God has evaporated.' She described to me how the future stretched before her like a long, grey, pointless, uphill struggle. 'I am finished. I've had enough.'

The exiles felt they had come to the end of the line. 'We are dried up,' they complained. 'We have no hope for the future.' Initially false prophets had told them they would soon be home, but years had gone by and news had come that Jerusalem, the place that Yahweh favoured, was destroyed. It was the final nail in the coffin of hope.

It was now, when all seemed lost, that Ezekiel came with a word of promise. Our earlier readings give the impression that he was very harsh, but here he brings encouragement. The people felt dry and helpless? Well, God was going to give them flesh and bones. His word and his Spirit were going to breathe new life into them. This scattered people would be like a united army, and he would bring them home.

Sometimes God can rescue us only when we are desperate. Sometimes we need to come to the end of all our efforts and resolutions before he can do his work in us. Sometimes it is only in recognising our own inadequacy that we make room for him to bathe us with his sufficiency.

Feeling empty and lost is very frightening, yet God specialises in filling the empty and finding the lost. Resurrection is his delight. Rest in him and trust him to do it in his time.

....

Lord, breathe your Spirit into the dead places of my life. Renew me by your word. I'm desperate.

You could use the words of Psalm 63 to express your longing and praise to God.

FB

In exile, await re-creation

This is what the Lord says—he who created you, Jacob, he who formed you, Israel: 'Do not fear, for I have redeemed you... See, I am doing a new thing! ... I provide water... to my people, my chosen, the people I formed for myself that they may proclaim my praise.'

Martha concluded that God had been good to her. Naturally bright, pretty and charming, she sailed through life. She secured a lucrative job in marketing, joined a church, chose a husband, produced a child and settled down to life in suburbia. All was well—at least, until she had a heart attack in her 30s, and witnessed the disintegration of her marriage and the loss of her son in a bitter custody battle. Unable to keep up with the demands of her work, she retreated to her parents' home to convalesce, her world in shreds.

It was there, as she contemplated the tatters of her life, that she had the time to take up painting. As she grew stronger, this hobby became a passion. As she created pictures from a soul that felt empty, God formed a new direction for her life. Today she is a well-respected artist, using her marketing skills to sell her work far and wide. And somewhere in each picture, three birds fly: Father, Son and Holy Spirit, who made something out of nothing.

The exiles had lost everything: their sense of identity as God's people, their place of worship, their homes and their farms. So God's word through Isaiah was astounding. Again and again, he spoke the Genesis word 'create'. In the wreck of a dispirited nation, God's Spirit was recreating. He was doing new things. What new things? Today, we owe thanks to the exiles for much of the Old Testament. It was at this time of crisis that the story of God's dealings with his people was gathered, recorded and interpreted. The struggle to understand what had happened led to a deeper theology. Synagogue worship developed in the absence of a temple. Something grew out of nothing.

....

Thank you, Creator God, that you can form something out of nothing. By your grace, no experience is ever wasted. Please renew me by your Spirit!

Read more of God's beautiful recreation promises in Isaiah 44:1–5.

FB

Jean Watson writes:

Who do you think you are? How well do you know yourself? And does self-knowledge matter? Because I think it does, I want to have a look at some Bible people and the impact of their characters within God's plans.

There's a very old saying that goes like this:

Sow a thought and you reap an act,
Sow an act and you reap a habit,
Sow a habit and you reap a character,
Sow a character and you reap a destiny.
CHARLES READE (1814–84)

That's putting it a bit simplistically and starkly, maybe, but I think it expresses a general truth about actions and consequences and about the way we, as individuals, affect the course of our own and other people's lives.

Back to our question: Does self-knowledge matter? Yes, because knowing ourselves means we can be more consistent and thoughtful in our choices and actions, as well as more understanding of others. These benefits cannot fail to have positive consequences. Within God's plans, they can alter the course of our own and other people's lives and futures for good—and for eternity.

So let's have a look at some Bible people and think about our own characters and characteristics and their potential impact.

Impulsive Peter

'What about you?' [Jesus asked]. 'Who do you say I am?' Peter
answered, 'You are the Messiah.'

I love impulsive Peter. In today's passage we see him being impulsively right and impulsively wrong. 'Who do you say I am?' Jesus asks
his disciples. Predictably, Peter answers first: 'You are the Messiah.'
Spot on, Peter!

Then Jesus predicts his death and Peter rebukes him. In Matthew's
account, he says, 'Never, Lord! This shall never happen to you!' (Matthew 16:22). It's an impulsive response, but this time Peter gets it
badly wrong and Jesus tells him so quite sharply. It's essential for the
disciples to grasp what he has just told them. (They don't—until later.)

Can you think of other examples of Peter's impulsiveness, right or
wrong? One of my favourites (in John 13) is when Jesus washes the
disciples' feet and Peter tries to refuse the service, feeling that he is
not worthy of it. But when Jesus replies that unless he carries out this
action, Peter will have no part with him, Peter responds, 'Not just
my feet but my hands and my head as well!' How human and how
endearing!

Other snapshots that spring to my mind include Peter recognising his sinfulness and falling at Jesus' feet (Luke 5:8); walking on the
water until his faith and his feet wobble (Matthew 14:30); blurting
out, at Jesus' transfiguration, 'It's good for us to be here! Let us put
up three shelters' (Mark 9:5); cutting off the ear of one of the people
trying to arrest Jesus (John 18:10); vowing never to desert Jesus, then
denying that he knew Jesus, and weeping bitterly (Matthew 26:33,
74–75).

Peter was flawed, like all of us. He doesn't always think before he
speaks or acts, but there is no doubting his good intentions, his sor-
row when he is wrong and his warm heart.

....

*What is your dominant characteristic? Reflect on its positive and,
perhaps, negative aspects and effects as you have experienced them.*

JW

Peter: sow a character, reap a destiny

'This is how God fulfilled what he had foretold through all the prophets, saying that his Messiah would suffer. Repent, then, and turn to God, so that your sins may be wiped out.'

How much Peter has grown! He heals a lame man with quiet authority in Jesus' name, then tells the whole crowd that it is by Jesus' power that the man has been healed. Then he gives a clear message about Jesus' life, death and resurrection and urges a response from his listeners.

The man who rebuked Jesus for saying that he must suffer is now explaining why Jesus had to suffer. The man who denied Jesus is now openly witnessing for him. Peter's impulsiveness is still in place but is tempered by what he has learnt through suffering and reflection. Now all his qualities of character can be used in the building of God's kingdom on earth.

What would you include in a list of Peter's qualities? His love for Jesus comes first, for me. Then there are his qualities of leadership, insight, warm-heartedness and humility—his capacity for recognising when he is wrong, deeply grieving over it and repenting of it. I am sure there are others you can think of.

What were the effects of his character within God's plan? If we think of his part in establishing the early church and of his contribution of biblical writings (Mark's Gospel—said to be at least partly Peter's account—and the letters 1 and 2 Peter), we can say that they were very far-reaching indeed.

Tradition has it that he was crucified, like Jesus, but upside down. I am sure he did not doubt his eternal destiny, and his influence certainly lives on in many lives.

....

Read John 21:15–19 to see what it shows about Peter's character. Now try rereading it as though Jesus were addressing his questions to you rather than to Peter. Reflect in God's presence on your responses and feelings.

JW

Martha: down-to-earth and practical

'Martha, Martha,' the Lord answered, 'you are worried and upset about many things, but few things are needed—or indeed only one.'

The scene is so easy to identify with, isn't it? Martha is bustling about, getting a meal served up for her guest, and catches sight of her sister apparently doing nothing. 'Can't you see how busy I am?' she asks Jesus. 'Tell Mary to help me.'

Have a look at Jesus' reply. What does it mean? Is this story telling us that people like Mary are better than people like Martha? I don't believe so. To be a hospitable, down-to-earth, practical person is perfectly acceptable. Such people are much needed and should be valued.

What I believe Jesus was indicating here was that there are times in life when the urgent has to be put aside temporarily so that we can attend to the truly important. At that time on that day in Mary's and Martha's home, the really important matter was giving one's whole attention to Jesus, listening to him. Everything else was relatively unimportant, and anything that got in the way of doing that or causing anyone to miss out on it would be deeply regretted.

Often, we only know how important an event was after it has happened. Then we're delighted if we 'caught' it and full of regret if we didn't. But Jesus was able to tell Mary and Martha at the time what their top priority needed to be—so they were indeed fortunate. I wonder whether Martha got the point then, or only later.

Many people didn't get the point—didn't understand how important Jesus was. I think of Jesus' anguished cry, 'If you... had only known on this day what would bring you peace...' as he entered Jerusalem for the last time (Luke 19:42).

....

Reflect in God's presence on whether, by exercising any of your worthwhile qualities, you are missing out on any important priorities; or whether any of your 'to do' lists could lead to some regretful 'If only's in your life.

JW

Mary: dreamy and intuitive

Mary... fell at his feet and said, 'Lord, if you had been here, my brother would not have died.'

We are not told much about the character of Mary, so I could be wrong in seeing her as dreamy and intuitive, just on the strength of her sitting at Jesus' feet and listening to what he said (Luke 10:39), and of her being different from Martha. I think there is more evidence of Martha's character. In yesterday's passage, she busied herself with cooking and serving a meal. In today's passage, when Jesus asks for the stone to be taken away from Lazarus' grave, it is Martha who objects: 'But... by this time there is a bad odour, for he has been there four days' (v. 39).

This passage shows us that both practical Martha and intuitive Mary—if that's what she was like—loved their brother. They also loved Jesus and believed that he was the Messiah. They trusted that if he had been with them, he would have healed their brother of his sickness and not allowed him to die.

Yet neither Martha's practical nature nor Mary's intuitive one could prepare them for what Jesus was going to do. His power was far greater than Mary could have imagined it to be. Perhaps his tears surprised her as they surprised the other people there. How much he must have loved Lazarus, they thought. But what he did would surprise them all even more. He called Lazarus out of the grave and brought him back to life and to his loved ones.

On a dreadful day after my husband's sudden death, I read this passage—and the words that Jesus spoke to Lazarus lit up for me. No, Jesus did not call my husband back to our life together, but I felt suddenly assured that he had called him back to a better, fuller life. This 'knowledge'—some might call it intuitive or faith-knowledge—brought comfort in amid the anguish of loss.

....

Are you more like Mary or Martha? Thank God that he knows and loves us just as we are, while helping us, if we are willing, to change and grow into the person he wants us to become in his plans.

JW

Esther: courageous and discerning

Mordecai… sent back this answer: '… If you remain silent at this time, relief and deliverance for the Jews will arise from another place… And who knows but that you have come to royal position for such a time as this?'

In this chapter, Mordecai tries to persuade Esther to help their people, the Jews, and Esther agrees to do so. What do you think it reveals about her character? Just to set the chapter in context: about 2500 years ago, the Jews were in exile in Persia when Xerxes was the despotic monarch. One of his court officials had persuaded him, with the promise of more money for his treasury, to sign a decree that all the Jews in his country would be massacred on a certain date.

Esther had been made queen but, instructed by her cousin, who had taken care of her since her parents' deaths, she had not revealed that she was Jewish. When Mordecai asked her to intervene with the king of behalf of her people, she courageously agreed to do so, knowing that it could lead to her death.

Throughout history, there have been people with a sense of destiny about a situation, who have had the courage to do whatever they believed was required of them in it. Martin Luther, the Protestant reformer, was one such person. When asked to deny his understanding of salvation, he said, 'Here I stand. I can do no other.' Esther said, 'I will go to the king, even if it is against the law. And if I perish, I perish' (v. 16). Perhaps she too had a sense of destiny in response to Mordecai's words.

I have had some 'I can do no other' times in my life, although not on anything like the same scale as Esther's moment of destiny. One involved a decision about whom I should marry and another about a course of training I could take. These led to changes in my life and the lives of others, both at the time and in the future.

....

Reflect on any similar moments you have faced. If you are facing one now, pray for the courage and discernment to say 'yes' or 'no' according to what would be right for you and others now.

JW

Esther: sow a character, reap a destiny

The king again asked, 'Queen Esther, what is your petition? It will be given you. What is your request? Even up to half the kingdom, it will be granted.' Then Queen Esther answered, 'If I have found favour with you, Your Majesty, and if it pleases you, grant me my life—this is my petition. And spare my people—this is my request.'

What aspects of Esther's character came to the fore in yesterday's passage? First, there was her courage—but it wasn't courage based on ignorance and lack of imagination. Esther knew the risk of going into the presence of a despotic and unpredictable king without an invitation. She was understandably and very humanly nervous, but her love and loyalty for Mordecai and for the Jewish people overcame her fear. I think I can add that her faith in God came into the picture. Although God is not mentioned by name in this book, Esther asks Mordecai to ask the people to fast for her, and this implies fervent and committed prayer to God.

Earlier in the book, we read, 'Esther had a lovely figure and was beautiful… Esther won the favour of everyone who saw her' (2:7, 15). In this chapter we see that she has brains and imagination as well as beauty and popularity. Knowing what the king is like, she invites him to a meal and makes him feel cosseted and comfortable before asking him, cleverly, to spare her life and the life of her people. The king can hardly refuse such a request in such a context.

Esther's whole being and character came into play, within God's plans, in saving her people from being massacred. (Sadly, the Jews' revenge, described in chapter 9, runs counter to later biblical injunctions about not taking revenge and about loving our enemies.)

....

What are your qualities of character? Thank God for the qualities you are grateful for and tell him about those that give you trouble. Offer yourself to God as a 'living sacrifice' (Romans 12:1). In his plans, who you are can affect others for great good.

JW

David: lovingly obedient

David said to the Philistine, 'You come against me with sword and spear and javelin, but I come against you in the name of the Lord Almighty… whom you have defied.'

Everyone enjoys David-and-Goliath stories—when the seemingly strong and inviolable are overcome by the comparatively weak and young. As you read the story, notice David's likable qualities. He tells King Saul, respectfully but quite naturally, about his experiences as a shepherd, guarding his sheep against wild animals—but he doesn't boast. He asserts that the Lord has rescued him in the past and will rescue him from the 'uncircumcised Philistine' (vv. 34–37). He is brave and full of faith, ready to defend the honour of God and the honour of God's people. Young as he is, he has learnt from his past experience and is prepared to go forward in faith on the strength of it.

All these things remained true as David matured, but to learn more about his character we need to read further. The friendship between David and Jonathan shows us David's capacity for loyal friendship, not just to Jonathan but to his crippled son (1 Samuel 20; 2 Samuel 9). His relationship with Bathsheba shows us that he was a man of strong emotions, capable of doing great wrong (committing adultery and causing the death of Bathsheba's husband), but also repenting and grieving deeply when convicted of his misdeeds (2 Samuel 11; Psalm 51).

David was a soldier as well as a poet and musician, a leader to whom others willingly submitted but who willingly himself submitted to God. Why do you think he is described as 'a man after God's heart' (1 Samuel 13:14)? Perhaps the following verses help with the answer: 'I have found David son of Jesse, a man after my own heart; he will do everything I want him to do' (Acts 13:22); and 'I desire to do your will, my God; your law is within my heart' (Psalm 40:8).

....

Reflect on the qualities suggested by these verses in relation to David's character and your own.

JW

A new home

'I will make you into a great nation and I will bless you; I will make your name great, and you will be a blessing. I will bless those who bless you, and whoever curses you I will curse; and all peoples on earth will be blessed through you.'

By the time you read this, our daughter will have finished school *(writes Catherine Butcher)*. Gradually she will become more inde-pendent until one day, God willing, she leaves home altogether. I don't look forward to that day. Our relationship will change. Although we will always be there for her as parents, she was given to us only for a season, to prepare her to take her place as an adult in God's world.

When she set off on a Duke of Edinburgh's Award hike earlier this year, I had a taste of what might come. It was cold and wet. She was sad and lonely, and all I could do was text encouragement and pray. My instinct was to jump into the car and rescue her, but she had important lessons to learn. As well as facing the physical challenges, she learned to praise God through the loneliness, tiredness and pain, reminding herself of God's presence and unwavering love. When the time comes for her to leave home, those lessons will be vital.

Abram faced a tough call: 'Leave your country, your people and your father's household and go to the land I will show you' (v. 1). Abram chose to obey God and left a comfortable city life, his family and friends, to find a new home in unknown territory. All he had was the promise that God would bless him and make him a blessing.

How do you respond in tough times—run for comfort or choose to obey God? I set my computer password to a challenge such as 'PraiseHim' or 'Rejoice!' so that every time I start work I'm reminded to look to God, not my circumstances. What daily tasks could you adapt to remind you to look to God? As always, Jesus is our example, 'who for the joy set before him endured the cross' (Hebrews 12:2).

....

Count your blessings, thanking God for what he has done for you in the past and asking for his help to focus on Jesus, whatever circumstances you face. If times are tough, expect to grow spiritual muscles.

CB

Under pressure

The Lord said to Abram after Lot had parted from him, '... Go, walk through the length and breadth of the land, for I am giving it to you.'

When we're under pressure, it's easy to lose sight of our goals. History records countless stories of people who failed again and again, but are now remembered for their greatness, not their failures. In her book *Never Give Up*, Joyce Meyer writes, 'The great dancer and movie star Fred Astaire took a screen test at MGM studios in 1933. A studio memo reported he was slightly bald, could not act, and could dance a little.' Discouragement didn't make him give up his goal.

Abram wasn't good at keeping on track when facing difficulties. He had arrived in Canaan with the promise that God would give the land to him. He'd been called to leave his father's household, but he'd brought his nephew Lot with him—and, when there was famine in Canaan, he left for Egypt, where he distorted the truth to protect himself. Abram did what seemed best in his own eyes, and God didn't speak to him again until he was back in Canaan and had separated from Lot. Then God underlined his amazing promise and told Abram to explore the land that had been promised to him.

Which of God's promises stand out for you? Have you explored the length and breadth of what God has promised? When Paul prayed for the Christians in Ephesus, he prayed that they would understand the dimensions of God's love for them—'to grasp how wide and long and high and deep is the love of Christ' (Ephesians 3:18). We could each spend a lifetime discovering the truth of that prayer. If you can appreciate how much God loves you, every aspect of your life will be transformed. Would Abram have resorted to lying to protect himself if he had really understood that God was in control of his life and would fulfil his promises?

....

Father, help me to explore the dimensions of your love through all of the joys, sorrows and challenges that life brings.

Make Paul's prayer in Ephesians 3:14–21 your own, for yourself and for those you love.

CB

God's work

'Do not be afraid, Abram. I am your shield, your very great reward.' … Abram believed the Lord, and he credited it to him as righteousness.

The famous Frank Sinatra song 'I did it my way!' could be Abram's own anthem. He found it difficult to grasp that he didn't have to work out his own future to fulfil the promises God had given him. All he had to do was to believe God. God would do the rest.

In chapter 15 we listen in on a dialogue between God and Abram. Like most of us, Abram has trouble believing God. He wants assurance. God explains clearly, 'A son coming from your own body will be your heir' (v. 4); Abram didn't have to do anything except trust God. You can imagine Sarai's mind working: 'Did God say "a son from Abram's body"? Did he mention who the mother would be?' True to the custom of the day, Sarai, who had not been able to conceive, gave her servant to Abram. They took matters into their own hands to ensure that Abram had an heir.

I wonder how many miracles we prevent or delay by trying to work out God's plans ourselves. How many problems could be avoided if only we let go, and let God take control? Abram's vision demonstrated vividly that God was the one both to initiate and to fulfil his plans.

With the benefit of hindsight, we can see the centuries of conflict in the Middle East between Ishmael's descendants and those of his brother Isaac.

Are there areas of your life that you are holding back from God? Do you believe wholeheartedly that God is in control, or are you still living your own way, letting doubt and fear limit you? Go back to yesterday's prayer and remind yourself of God's love for you. Ask God to help you learn to recognise his guidance in every aspect of life.

....

'When we walk with the Lord in the light of his word, what a glory he sheds on our way! While we do his good will, he abides with us still, and with all who will trust and obey.'

JOHN H. SAMMIS (1846–1919)

CB

Testing, testing

'The fire and wood are here,' Isaac said, 'but where is the lamb for the burnt offering?' Abraham answered, 'God himself will provide the lamb.' … So Abraham called that place The Lord Will Provide.

Isaac is finally born when Abraham is 100 and Sarah is 90. God's promise will be fulfilled—but only if Isaac goes on to have children of his own. Obedience didn't come naturally to Abraham (as Abram is now known). He has learnt the hard way to trust and obey God. This time, when God tells him to sacrifice his only son, Abraham does exactly what God says, step by step, without resorting to his own solutions or going his own way. He has learnt to rely on God utterly and to listen carefully to his voice, obeying without running ahead. He says confidently, 'God himself will supply the lamb for the burnt offering.' Then, when the angel calls to him to stop, he stops, and God provides a scapegoat—the forerunner of Jesus, who takes our place as the perfect, once-for-all sacrifice.

Trusting and obeying God in everything is not easy, but Jesus made a direct connection between obeying and loving. 'If you love me, you will obey what I command,' he said. To help us to know what God wants, he promised, 'I will ask the Father, and he will give you another Counsellor to be with you for ever—the Spirit of truth' (John 14:15–17). God does not intend our lives to be a testing and guessing game, trying to follow the dictates of a harsh, remote deity. Instead, as he did with Abraham, he loves us and perseveres with us, expanding our capacity to trust him, giving us his Holy Spirit to teach us how to live God's way. As Jesus said, 'When he, the Spirit of truth, comes, he will guide you into all truth' (John 16:13). So we can be confident in giving our lives completely to God. He will guide us and guard us, doing what is best for us, as a Father who loves us enough to give his only Son to rescue us from the consequences of our mistakes.

....

'All to Jesus I surrender; Lord, I give myself to Thee;
Fill me with Thy love and power; Let Thy blessing fall on me.'
Judson W. Van De Venter (1896)

. CB

Subscription Information

Each issue of *Day by Day with God* is available from Christian bookshops everywhere. Copies may also be available through your church Book Agent or from the person who distributes Bible reading notes in your church.

Alternatively you may obtain *Day by Day with God* on subscription direct from the publishers. There are two kinds of subscription:

Individual Subscriptions are for four copies or less, and include postage and packing. To order an annual Individual Subscription, please complete the details on page 142 and send the coupon with payment to BRF in Abingdon. You can also use the form to order a Gift Subscription for a friend.

Church Subscriptions are for five copies or more, sent to one address, and are supplied post free. Church Subscriptions run from 1 May to 30 April each year and are invoiced annually. To order a Church Subscription, please complete the details opposite and send the coupon to BRF in Abingdon. You will receive an invoice with the first issue of notes.

All subscription enquiries should be directed to:

BRF
15 The Chambers
Vineyard
Abingdon
OX14 3FE

Tel: 01865 319700
Fax: 01865 319701
E-mail: subscriptions@brf.org.uk

Church Subscriptions

The Church Subscription rate for *Day by Day with God* will be £12.15 per person until April 2012.

❏ I would like to take out a church subscription for _____ (Qty) copies.

❏ Please start my order with the September 2011 / January 2012 / May 2012* issue. I would like to pay annually/receive an invoice with each edition of the notes*.
(*Please delete as appropriate)

Please do not send any money with your order. Send your order to BRF and we will send you an invoice. The Church Subscription year is from May to April. If you start subscribing in the middle of a subscription year we will invoice you for the remaining number of issues left in that year.

Name and address of the person organising the Church Subscription:

Name_____

Address_____

_____

Postcode _____ Telephone _____

Church _____

Name of Minister _____

Name and address of the person paying the invoice if the invoice needs to be sent directly to them:

Name_____

Address_____

_____

Postcode _____ Telephone _____

Please send your coupon to:

BRF
15 The Chambers
Vineyard
Abingdon
Oxon
OX14 3FE

❏ Please do not send me further information about BRF publications

Individual Subscriptions

❏ I would like to give a gift subscription (please complete both name and address sections below)

❏ I would like to take out a subscription myself (complete your name and address details only once)

Your name _____

Your address _____

_____ Postcode _____

Tel _____ Email _____

Gift subscription name _____

Gift subscription address _____

_____ Postcode _____

Gift message (20 words max) _____

_____

Please send *Day by Day with God* for one year, beginning with the September 2011 / January 2012 / May 2012 issue: (delete as applicable)

	UK	Surface	Air Mail
Day by Day with God	❏ £15.15	❏ £17.25	❏ £20.25
2-year subscription	❏ £27.00	N/A	N/A

Please complete the payment details below and send your coupon, with appropriate payment, to BRF, 15 The Chambers, Vineyard, Abingdon, Oxon OX14 3FE

Total enclosed £ _____ (cheques should be made payable to 'BRF')

Please charge my Visa ❏ Mastercard ❏ Switch card ❏ with £ _____

Card no. ⬜⬜⬜⬜⬜⬜⬜⬜⬜⬜⬜⬜⬜⬜⬜⬜

Expires ⬜⬜⬜⬜ Security code ⬜⬜⬜

Issue no (Switch) ⬜⬜⬜⬜

Signature _____
(essential if paying by credit/Switch card)

NB: These notes are also available from Christian bookshops everywhere.

❏ Please do not send me further information about BRF publications

DBDWG0211   BRF is a Registered Charity

Christina Press Publications Order Form

All of these publications are available from Christian bookshops everywhere or, in case of difficulty, direct from the publisher. Please make your selection below, complete the payment details and send your order with payment as appropriate to:

Christina Press Ltd, 17 Church Road, Tunbridge Wells, Kent TN1 1LG

		Qty	Price	Total
8700	God's Catalyst	____	£8.99	____
8701	Women Celebrating Faith	____	£5.99	____
8702	Precious to God	____	£5.99	____
8703	Angels Keep Watch	____	£5.99	____
8704	Life Path	____	£5.99	____
8705	Pathway Through Grief	____	£6.99	____
8706	Who'd Plant a Church?	____	£5.99	____
8707	Dear God, It's Me and It's Urgent	____	£6.99	____
8708	Not a Super-Saint	____	£6.99	____
8709	The Addiction of a Busy Life	____	£5.99	____
8710	In His Time	____	£5.99	____

POSTAGE AND PACKING CHARGES				
	UK	Europe	Surface	Air Mail
£7.00 & under	£1.25	£3.00	£3.50	£5.50
£7.10–£29.99	£2.25	£5.50	£6.50	£10.00
£30.00 & over	free	prices on request		

Total cost of books   £ ____
Postage and Packing   £ ____
TOTAL   £ ____

All prices are correct at time of going to press, are subject to the prevailing rate of VAT and may be subject to change without prior warning.

Name _____

Address _____

_____ Postcode _____

Total enclosed £ _____ (cheques should be made payable to 'Christina Press Ltd')

❑ Please do not send me further information about Christina Press publications

DBDWG0211

Other BRF titles

Time for Reflection Ann Persson (£6.99)
It is not easy to switch from activity to stillness, from doing to being in the presence of God. This book of biblically rooted meditations provides accessible and practical routes to exploring prayer as that way of being in God's presence. Loosely based around the seasons of the Church year and also drawing inspiration from the seasons of nature, the meditations range from short 'spaces for grace' to longer exercises that can form the basis for a personal quiet day or retreat.

Writing the Icon of the Heart Maggie Ross (£7.99)
We are invited to share the reflections of one who, over the years, has spent long hours in silence and prayer in one of the world's most wild and solitary landscapes, as well as the more urban context of Oxford. Casting new and often startling light on ancient texts and long-established spiritual practices, Maggie Ross shows how faith cannot be divorced from an outlook characterised by a rigorous questioning and testing of assumptions, and a passionate concern for the created world in which we are blessed to live.

Pilgrimage Andrew Jones (£8.99)
At a time when the Church seems increasingly exiled and estranged from our culture, more and more people are treading the ancient pilgrim routes, whether they are committed Christians, spiritual seekers or simply curious. In this book, Andrew Jones shows how pilgrimage has the power to awaken those at all stages of belief to remembering the story of God's creating and redeeming work in history, the story that tells us who we are, where we have come from and where we are going. The book concludes with a focus on eight popular places of pilgrimage in the British Isles, drawing out lessons from their history and spiritual heritage.

Quiet Spaces: Bread for the journey Ed. Heather Fenton (£4.99)
In this issue we are tasting some good food of the word of God, and our focus will be on bread. Among the good things set out on the table is Thomas O'Loughlin's exploration of Jesus calling himself 'the bread of life'—one of the 'I am' phrases found in John's Gospel. Elsewhere Heather Fenton enables us to think about 'Bethlehem: the house of bread'. Recipes, ideas, worship material, new insights are all here, encouraging us in our own journey and giving us the strength to go on.

These titles are available from your local Christian bookshop. Alternatively, you can order from our website, www.brfonline.org.uk.

FREE!

4 Books
and a surprise gift!

We would like to take this opportunity to thank you for reading this Mills & Boon® book by offering you the chance to take FOUR more specially selected titles from the Modern Romance™ series absolutely FREE! We're also making this offer to introduce you to the benefits of the Reader Service™—

- ★ FREE home delivery
- ★ FREE gifts and competitions
- ★ FREE monthly Newsletter
- ★ Exclusive Reader Service offers
- ★ Books available before they're in the shops

Accepting these FREE books and gift places you under no obligation to buy, you may cancel at any time, even after receiving your free shipment. Simply complete your details below and return the entire page to the address below. You don't even need a stamp!

YES! Please send me 4 free Modern Romance books and a surprise gift. I understand that unless you hear from me, I will receive 6 superb new titles every month for just £2.69 each, postage and packing free. I am under no obligation to purchase any books and may cancel my subscription at any time. The free books and gift will be mine to keep in any case.

P4ZEF

Ms/Mrs/Miss/Mr ....Initials............................
BLOCK CAPITALS PLEASE

Surname ....

Address...

....

....Postcode ....

Send this whole page to:
UK: FREEPOST CN8I, Croydon, CR9 3WZ

Courage Bay... a community founded on bravery.
Meet the town's heroes – the people of
Courage Bay Emergency services.
Bold enough to risk their lives – and their hearts.

Available from 2nd January

Available at most branches of WH Smith, Tesco, ASDA, Martins, Borders,
Eason, Sainsbury's and all good paperback bookshops.

CODE RED/PREQUEL

MILLS & BOON

Volume 7
on sale from
2nd January
2005

Lynne
Graham

International Playboys

Crime of
Passion

On sale 7th January 2005

Available at most branches of WHSmith, Tesco, ASDA, Martins, Borders, Eason, Sainsbury's and all good paperback bookshops.

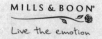

Modern
romance™

THE BILLIONAIRE BOSS'S BRIDE by Cathy Williams

On her first day as PA to Curtis Diaz, Tessa makes a bad impression on her sexy boss. It sparks a turbulent business relationship – and underneath passion is surging! Curtis wants to know why he desires Tessa like no other woman – and offers a proposition she can't refuse...

HIS PREGNANCY BARGAIN by Kim Lawrence

Megan knows that seeing sexy Lucas Patrick is wrong, but how else can she foil her mother's matchmaking? He pretends to be infatuated with her...then he decides to make his acting role real, and Megan finds herself in a bigger fix: she's pregnant!

THE BRUNELLESCI BABY by Daphne Clair

Ruthless Italian tycoon Zandro Brunellesci has decided his dead brother's child must be taken away from Lia - his brother's mistress would be an unsuitable mother. Yet she seems to have changed and Zandro even finds himself attracted to her...

THE ITALIAN'S MISTRESS by Melanie Milburne

When it comes to Anna Stockton, Lucio Ventressi wants only one thing – vengeance for the way she dumped him. Anna needs money and Lucio makes her an offer: he'll pay her to be his mistress for three months. Anna has no choice but to agree...

Don't miss out...

On sale 7th January 2005

Available at most branches of WHSmith, Tesco, ASDA, Martins, Borders, Eason, Sainsbury's and all good paperback bookshops.

and letting them hug him tightly even though he wondered if he'd ever breathe again. His *mama*'s eyes kept filling with tears. His *papa* kept kissing her. She said she was crying because she was so happy. How funny adults were, he thought. And snuggled contentedly between them by the pool, wondering if this was a good time to ask for a baby brother or sister to play with.